knitting
goes
large

knitting goes
large

20 designs to flatter your figure

SHARON BRANT

with
JENNIE ATKINSON
WENDY BAKER
KIM HARGREAVES
MARTIN STOREY

photography by
JOHN HESELTINE

St. Martin's Griffin
New York

Editor Sally Harding
Designer Anne Wilson
Photographer John Heseltine
Styling Louise Sykes and Susan Berry
Pattern writer Sue Whiting
Pattern checker Emma King
Diagrams Lisa Richardson

Associate Publisher Susan Berry

Library of Congress Cataloging-in-Publication Data Available Upon Request

ISBN-13: 978-0-312-54010-4
ISBN-10: 0-312-54010-8

First Edition: January 2009

10 9 8 7 6 5 4 3 2 1

contents

introduction

My awareness of the needs of larger women comes from my personal experience as a "big girl." Without giving away any trade secrets, I am larger than average! As a knitter, hand knit designer and Rowan's Retail Manager, I get a lot of large ladies approaching me to ask for more knitting patterns for women with full figures. And they aren't shy about offering advice on the sweater styles they are looking for. What seems to irritate them most of all is the ever-expanding array of knitting patterns on offer that cater exclusively for skinny women—and the fact that they are modeled on even skinnier ones!

I have put this collection of knitwear together for women with generous curves who are looking for stylish hand knits designed with them in mind. There are a variety of necklines, garment shapes, lengths, collars, and knitting details—such as Fair Isle and cables—to choose

RIGHT These two models show how different our body shapes can be. They both wear the same dress size (size 14–16), but because of their different heights and personal curves, the garment shapes they choose to flatter their figures will not be the same. Their shapes also illustrate how no one fits neatly into store sizes. Model A is shorter, but has a longer body length than Model B. Model B has a longer neck than Model A. Their hips, waists, and bottoms curve in and out to different degrees and at different levels. All these factors play a part in the sweater shape that suits each woman best.

Model A   **Model B**

from, plus a few accessories. The five designers (Jennie Atkinson, Wendy Baker, Kim Hargreaves, Martin Storey, and Catherine Tough) whose work I have chosen to include have differing styles to cover a wide range of tastes. So hopefully there are several patterns within this selection to tempt every big beautiful knitter out there.

Before leafing through the patterns to find one to knit, take the time to read my short introduction. I have a few good tips on how to choose the sweater that complements your shape and suits your personal sense of style, and how to adjust your garment to fit you perfectly. If you follow my advice, you will be able to knit something that you will wear over and over and never get sick of—because it feels and looks just right for you.

GARMENT SHAPES THAT FLATTER CURVACEOUS WOMEN

I am a firm believer that, whatever your size or shape, you need to play to your strengths and play down what you consider your "problem areas." We big women are not all big in the same places, so one size or one style does definitely not "fit all" (see Models A and B left).

When designing or knitting for, or even dressing as, a larger lady the garment shape you choose will depend on where the biggest curves are in your figure. You can then decide which curves are an asset and which you want to play down—whether to accentuate them or cover them up. Choosing knitwear that will successfully either enhance or detract from aspects of your full figure is one of the most important things to focus on when deciding which pattern to knit.

STEP-BY-STEP TO FINDING THE BEST GARMENT SHAPE FOR YOU

Spend some time with a long mirror and your wardrobe, so you can analyze which garment shape will suit you best. You don't want to rush the process. Make sure you have at least a couple hours to spare. Ask a friend to join you; she can pin your clothes as needed and offer her opinion on the shapes that flatter your curves.

Follow these simple guidelines to choose a shape you are comfortable with:

- Try some of your clothes on and decide what you feel happy and confident in.

- Decide which of the garment shapes you have chosen seems to suit you best—it doesn't have to be a knitted garment. Put it on and stand in front of the mirror.

- Now ask yourself the following:
  Is it the right length?
  Are the sleeves the right length?
  What sort of sleeve style does it have (fitted, drop shoulder)?
  Does it have shaping along the side seams?

- Having answered these questions, consider what might make the shape even more perfect for you. Perhaps you would like to add or subtract an inch to the body or sleeve length. If the garment has drop shoulders (something large women should avoid), try lifting the shoulder and pinning it into an armhole shape to see the difference—you will loose pounds in seconds! If the garment has shaping at the side seam, it will flatter your curves as long as the sweater isn't clinging.

DECIDING ON THE RIGHT SWEATER LENGTH

Now your are ready to find a garment in the book that resembles the shape you are looking for. While you are deciding, consider the following:

- It's worthwhile thinking about what you will be wearing your sweater with. Try on some bottoms and tops in your wardrobe to get an idea of what type of sweater would suit them.

- If you were to wear a knitted top with an A-line skirt, for instance, it is better to opt for a shorter length of knitted top, as a long garment will join up with the widest part of the skirt and you will become one large box! The correct length would be to hip-bone level.

- If you intend to wear your knitted top with tight-fitting jeans or trousers, then you might like to aim for a longer sweater length. A shorter length may draw attention to a large tummy or bottom. I have a couple of sweaters that stop at my hip and I would only wear them with certain A-line skirts, I would never consider wearing them with trousers.

WHICH STYLE OF GARMENT FOR WHICH FIGURE SHAPE?

Once you decide which garment shape suits you best, consider what style will flatter you, paying particular attention to necklines. Again, think which curves you want to make the most of and which you want to hide or draw attention away from. Here are some do's and don'ts:

Large bust

Do's:

- If you have a large bust choose a low neckline, this will flatter you.
- Jackets or cardigans with a deep neckline are also flattering, if worn open.

Don'ts:

- Avoid tight, high necks as these will create a large expanse of fabric between your neck and tummy, exaggerating your bust size.

Large bottom/tummy

Do's:

- High necklines are good as are interesting necklines—they draw the eye away from the tummy area.
- Cover up the bottom/tummy area with a long sweater when wearing trousers.

Don'ts

- Avoid wearing sweaters that go below hip-level with an A-line skirt.

These are only a few suggestions. Remember that each of us has a unique body shape and a unique sense of style and taste. If you are still unsure about the garment style for you, why not try on styles in a store. You may find that a shape you have never tried before is just what you are looking for! Don't be afraid to take a tape measure with you to measure flattering sleeve or body lengths, or widths across hips and bust.

OPPOSITE PAGE LEFT Low necklines flatter a large bust (left), as does a soft lace stole (see pages 104–107) draped gracefully over the shoulders.

OPPOSITE PAGE RIGHT Interesting necklines like the one on the hooded *Cabled Tunic* (see page 16) catch the eye and draw it away from a generous tummy or bottom.

ABOVE I recommend the long version of the *Swing Jacket* (see page 90) for a straightish full figure or a large bottom. The short version is great for ladies with smallish tops and large hips.

TOP RIGHT The *Seed Stitch Jacket* (see page 26) will suit many body shapes. It can be fastened with a decorative pin or left open depending on what flatters you most.

RIGHT Generous collars like the one on the *Large Collar Jacket* (see page 32) frame the face beautifully and can be flattering on short sweaters for large women.

DEVELOPING YOUR PERSONAL STYLE

Finding the sweater shape, length, and style that makes the most of your body shape will give you are great sense of achievement and confidence. It is the first big step in choosing the right garments to knit for your wardrobe. But don't stop there! The fun part of the exercise it going on to develop a unique dress style. You can do this by finding sweater details, textures, and colors that you love.

Although your sense of style will depend largely on your personal taste, always keep in mind what will enhance the appeal of your large form. And as knitters, of course, you will want to be knitting textures you enjoy knitting, in colors and yarns that you like the feel and look of.

Sweater details

When you are choosing a sweater pattern, look for subtle, stylish edgings. Knitted-in beads, frills, or rolled edgings around cuffs, the lower edge of the garment, and especially necklines will capture the viewer's eye. These details will draw attention away from large curves you may want to play down, and the big bonus is that they are fun to knit!

Sweater textures

If you love knitting textures, stick to the softer, more fluid ones like seed stitch, garter stitch, and fine cables that will drape softly around your curves. Denser, deep textures—such as huge cables—will add too much thickness to your figure, as will super-thick yarns.

ABOVE Elegant rolled edgings on the *Wrap Jacket* (see page 74) provide detailing that catches the eye. The silk and wool yarn drapes gracefully over body curves—always a plus on a full figure.

ABOVE Pick knitted textures carefully. It doesn't mean you can't knit cables if they are your favorite knitting technique! Just stick to fine ones like those on the *Twisted Rib Cardigan* (see page 122).

Choosing yarn colors

Larger ladies always want to drape themselves in black hoping it makes them look slimmer. Don't get me wrong, I am a lover of black, but I always use a splash of stylish color in detailing and accessories for eyecatching accents.

It's important to choose the right color for you; one that makes you glow. If you don't want the expense of going to a color consultant, you can "do it yourself." Get a couple of girlfriends to come over and help. First, cover yourself in a white sheet and stand in front of a mirror in a natural light. Then drape colors on your shoulders—garments or even balls of yarn—and watch your face change. It will become evident which colors make you glow and which make you look like you need to take some iron pills!

Once you discover the colors that suit you, don't think you need to cover yourself in them. Try using standard colors for the main part of the garment and then add small accents of your chosen color—for example, by casting on or binding off with this color.

Accessories for large ladies

Accessories are great for distracting attention away from those larger curves and provide a perfect way to use those brighter, stronger colors. Shawls, scarves, and long necklaces can make your shape appear narrower.

ABOVE You can choose a slimming dark color for the background shade on the *Fair Isle Sweater* (see page 62) and bring in bright or subtle contrasting colors—or a mixture of both—in the Fair Isle bands.

ABOVE If subdued shades suit your skin color and body shape best, introduce more exciting colors in your accessories as shown here with the beaded *Scarf* (see page 102) worn as a shawl over the shoulders.

CHOOSING WHICH SIZE TO KNIT

Hopefully, the advice on pages 6–11 will have helped you work out the sweater shape and style that you want to knit. Your next step is to choose which size to knit.

Taking body measurements

It is essential to take accurate bust and hip measurements before you start. The sweater patterns in this book are designed to fit different bust sizes. Start out by choosing the size that suits your bust size and then look at the finished knitted measurement around the bust. This shows how much "ease" is incorporated into the sweater around the bust, and it is also the measurement that needs to fit (without clinging) around your hips.

Measuring a garment that fits you best

Next, take the garment from your wardrobe that you chose earlier as the ideal shape and fit for you, and lay it out flat on the floor. Measure the width, garment length and sleeve length, and see if these match the finished sweater measurements in the size you have chosen.

Alternatively, if you only have a garment that is "almost right" but needs some alterations, put it on and ask a friend to take the desired measurements while you are wearing it. After having taken these measurements, you may decide to go up or down a sweater size to match the size more closely to your perfect fit and shape.

WORKING TO THE CORRECT GAUGE TO ENSURE A GOOD FIT

Having worked out which size is right for you, you need to make sure that your knitted pieces will match the finished knitted measurements given for this size. You can only do this if your gauge is the same as the one specified in the pattern. Take your time to get the correct gauge, changing to a smaller or larger needle size if necessary (see page 130 for more about gauge.)

MAKING SIMPLE PATTERN ADJUSTMENTS FOR A BETTER FIT

There are some simple pattern adjustments you can make to obtain an even better fit, to suit your unique figure shape. Avoid the more advanced alterations if you are a beginner knitter, or ask a skilled and experienced knitter for help in making your adjustments.

Altering sweater length

There are simple instructions on page 130 for how to lengthen a simple straight-sided garment shape. These instructions are easy to apply to a pattern that tells you to knit a certain number of inches (centimeters) before you reach the armhole. But if the instructions call for a certain number of rows to be worked to the armhole, you will need to make a calculation to find out how many extra (or fewer) rows to work.

For example, if the gauge for the garment is 28 rows to 4in/10cm, divide by 28 by 4 (or 10) to figure out how many rows to add per 1in (or 1cm)—7 rows per inch or 2.8 rows per centimeter. So to make your sweater 2in (5cm) longer, knit 14 rows more.

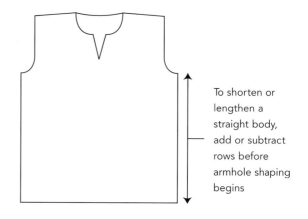

To shorten or lengthen a straight body, add or subtract rows before armhole shaping begins

Changing the length of a sweater that goes in at the waist is more difficult and should be left to very experienced knitters. To do this, you need to decide where you need more or less length—above or below the waist—then recalculate the positions of increases

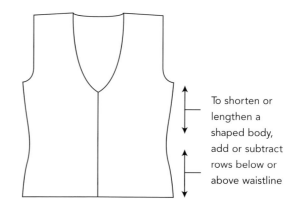

To shorten or lengthen a shaped body, add or subtract rows below or above waistline

and/or decreases. The is easiest way to do this is by charting the knitting on graph paper row by row.

Altering sweater width

The best way to get the right width for your sweater—one that will fit your bust and hips—is to choose the size in the pattern that matches your chosen width as closely as possible.

It may be, however, that a width big enough for your hips or tummy area is too large across your bust. If the discrepancy isn't too great, it is possible to make the top of the sweater 3/4–1in (2–2.5cm) narrower between the armholes without having to change the pattern too drastically. Don't, however, attempt this unless you are an experienced knitter! Take off a few extra stitches in each armhole shaping, and then when shaping the neck and shoulders spread these missing stitches out over these three sections—two shoulders and neck.

To change width across shoulders, distribute changes equally across three sections between armholes

Altering sleeve length

First of all, establish the length of sleeve you require. To achieve the best results, knit the front and back of the garment, baste them together and then try on this part of the garment. Now you can see exactly where the bottom of the armhole is going to fall on your body, and you can measure from there to where you want the bottom of the sleeve to come on your arm.

Once you have determined the length of sleeve you require, take off the length of the cuff if there is one. Then using the gauge provided for the garment, work

out how many rows there will be in the new sleeve length. Calculate how many times you have to increase at each end of the row in the sleeve instructions. Do this by subtracting the number of stitches there are before the increasing begins from the number of stitches you should have when all the increases are complete. Divide this by two for the number of increase rows you need. Now divide the number of rows in the sleeve by the number of increase rows—the answer shows approximately how many plain rows there should be between increase rows. Spread the increase rows out according to how you want the sleeve shaped—steeper increasing at the bottom of

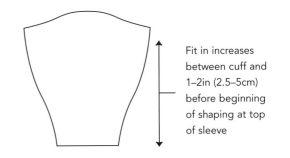

Fit in increases between cuff and 1–2in (2.5–5cm) before beginning of shaping at top of sleeve

the sleeve (increase rows closer together) and more gradual increasing at the top (increase rows farther apart). It is best to leave at least 1–2in (2.5–5cm) without shaping right before the beginning of the shaping at the top of sleeve—this is where you need the most ample width for comfort. Again, drawing your sleeve out on graph paper row by row is the easiest way to plan your increases; this is the trick designers use, as it eliminates the possibility of faulty calculations!

Hopefully this introduction to knitting for larger women will have started you off on your way to knitting a garment that will fit well and suit your shape—a garment that you will wear in comfort and confidence for many years. Happy knitting!

—Sharon Brant

projects

cabled tunic

MARTIN STOREY

TO FIT BUST

38	40	42	44	46	48	in
97	102	107	112	117	122	cm

FINISHED MEASUREMENTS

Around bust

46	48½	50½	52¼	54¼	56¼	in
117	123	128	133	138	143	cm

Length to shoulder

27½	28	28¼	28¾	29	29½	in
70	71	72	73	74	75	cm

Sleeve seam

17¼	17¼	17¾	17¾	17¾	17¾	in
44	44	45	45	45	45	cm

YARN

23 (24: 25: 26: 27: 28) x 1¾oz/102yd balls of Rowan *Denim* in Memphis 229

NEEDLES

Pair of size 3 (3.25mm) knitting needles
Pair of size 6 (4mm) knitting needles

Size 3 (3.25mm) circular knitting needle
Cable needle

GAUGE

Before washing: 23 sts and 28 rows to 4in/10cm measured over patt using size 6 (4mm) needles *or size to obtain correct gauge.*

SPECIAL NOTE

Rowan *Denim* shrinks in length when washed for the first time. Allowances have been made in the pattern for this shrinkage. The finished measurements given are those obtained after washing.

ABBREVIATIONS

See page 132.

SPECIAL ABBREVIATIONS

Tw2R = slip next st onto cable needle and leave at back of work, K1 tbl, then P1 from cable needle; **Tw2L** = slip next st onto cable needle and leave at front of work, P1, then K1 tbl from cable needle; **C3B** = slip next 2 sts onto cable needle and leave at back of work, K1, then K2 from cable needle; **C3F** = slip next st onto cable needle and leave at front of work, K2, then K1 from cable needle; **Cr3L** = slip next st onto cable needle and leave at front of work, K1 tbl, P1, then K1 tbl from cable needle.

BACK

Using size 3 (3.25mm) needles, cast on 117 (123: 129: 135: 141: 147) sts.
Row 1 (RS) K1, *P1, K1; rep from * to end.
Row 2 Rep row 1.

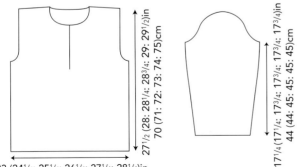

23 (24¼: 25¼: 26¼: 27¼: 28¼)in
58.5 (61.5: 64: 66.5: 69: 71.5)cm

27½ (28: 28¼: 28¾: 29: 29½)in
70 (71: 72: 73: 74: 75)cm

17¼ (17¼: 17¾: 17¾: 17¾: 17¾)in
44 (44: 45: 45: 45: 45)cm

These 2 rows form seed st.

Work in seed st for 7 rows more, ending with WS facing for next row.

Row 10 (WS) Seed st 27 (30: 33: 36: 39: 42) sts, *[M1, seed st 3 sts] twice, [M1, seed st 2 sts] 4 times, [M1, seed st 3 sts] twice, M1*, seed st 23 sts; rep from * to * once more, seed st to end. 135 (141: 147: 153: 159: 165) sts.

Change to size 6 (4mm) needles.

Now work in cable patt as follows:

Row 1 (RS) Seed st 26 (29: 32: 35: 38: 41) sts, *[P1, K1 tbl] twice, P3, K1 tbl, P1, K1 tbl, P2, K7, P2, K1 tbl, P1, K1 tbl, P3, [K1 tbl, P1] twice*, seed st 21 sts; rep from * to * once more, seed st to end.

Row 2 Seed st 26 (29: 32: 35: 38: 41) sts, *[K1, P1 tbl] twice, K3, P1 tbl, K1, P1 tbl, K2, P7, K2, P1 tbl, K1, P1 tbl, K3, [P1 tbl, K1] twice*, seed st 21 sts; rep from * to * once more, seed st to end.

Row 3 Seed st 26 (29: 32: 35: 38: 41) sts, *[P1, K1 tbl] twice, P3, K1 tbl, P1, K1 tbl, P2, C3B, K1, C3F, P2, K1 tbl, P1, K1 tbl, P3, [K1 tbl, P1] twice*, seed st 21 sts; rep from * to * once more, seed st to end.

Row 4 Rep row 2.

Row 5 Seed st 26 (29: 32: 35: 38: 41) sts, *P1, K1 tbl, P1, Tw2L, P1, Tw2R, P1, K1 tbl, P2, K7, P2, K1 tbl, P1, Tw2L, P1, Tw2R, P1, K1 tbl, P1*, seed st 21 sts; rep from * to * once more, seed st to end.

Row 6 Seed st 26 (29: 32: 35: 38: 41) sts, *K1, P1 tbl, K2, P1 tbl, K1, [P1 tbl, K2] twice, P7, [K2, P1 tbl] twice, K1, P1 tbl, K2, P1 tbl, K1*, seed st 21 sts; rep from * to * once more, seed st to end.

Row 7 Seed st 26 (29: 32: 35: 38: 41) sts, *P1, K1 tbl, P2, Cr3L, P2, K1 tbl, P2, C3B, K1, C3F, P2, K1 tbl, P2, Cr3L, P2, K1 tbl, P1*, seed st 21 sts; rep from * to * once more, seed st to end.

Row 8 Rep row 6.

Row 9 Seed st 26 (29: 32: 35: 38: 41) sts, *P1, K1 tbl, P1, Tw2R, P1, Tw2L, P1, K1 tbl, P2, K7, P2, K1 tbl, P1, Tw2R, P1, Tw2L, P1, K1 tbl, P1*, seed st 21 sts; rep from * to * once more, seed st to end.

Row 10 Rep row 2.

Row 11 Rep row 3.

Row 12 Rep row 2.

These 12 rows form patt.**

Work even in patt until Back measures 22 (22: 22½: 22½: 23: 23)in/56 (56: 57: 57: 58.5: 58.5)cm from cast-on edge, ending with RS facing for next row.

Shape armholes

Keeping patt correct, bind off 8 (8: 9: 9: 10: 10) sts at beg of next 2 rows. 119 (125: 129: 135: 139: 145) sts.

Dec 1 st at each end of next 5 (7: 7: 9: 9: 11) rows, then on foll 3 (3: 4: 4: 5: 5) alt rows, then on 2 foll 4th rows. 99 (101: 103: 105: 107: 109) sts.

Work even until armhole measures 10 (10½: 10½: 11: 11: 11½)in/25.5 (27: 27: 28: 28: 29)cm, ending with RS facing for next row.

Shape back neck and shoulders

Bind off 9 (10: 10: 10: 10: 11) sts at beg of next 2 rows. 81 (81: 83: 85: 87: 87) sts.

Next row (RS) Bind off 9 (10: 10: 10: 10: 11) sts, patt until there are 14 (13: 14: 14: 15: 14) sts on right needle and turn, leaving rem sts on a holder.

Work each side of neck separately.

Bind off 4 sts at beg of next row.

Bind off rem 10 (9: 10: 10: 11: 10) sts.

With RS facing, rejoin yarn to rem sts, bind off center 35 (35: 35: 37: 37: 37) sts, patt to end.

Complete to match first side, reversing shapings.

POCKET LININGS (make 2)

Using size 6 (4mm) needles, cast on 29 sts.

Starting with a K row, work in St st for 49 rows, ending with WS facing for next row.

Row 50 (WS) P4, [M1, P3] 7 times, M1, P4. 37 sts.

Break off yarn and leave sts on a holder.

FRONT

Work as given for Back to **.

Work in patt for 42 rows more, ending with RS facing for next row.

Place pockets

Next row (RS) Patt 20 (23: 26: 29: 32: 35) sts, slip next 37 sts onto a holder and, in their place, patt across 37 sts of first Pocket Lining, patt 21 sts, slip next 37 sts onto a holder and, in their place, patt across 37 sts of second Pocket Lining, patt to end.

Work even until 9 rows fewer have been worked than on Back to start of armhole shaping, ending with WS facing for next row.

Next row (WS) Patt 67 (70: 73: 76: 79: 82) sts, inc in next st, patt to end. 136 (142: 148: 154: 160: 166) sts.

Divide for front opening
Next row (RS) Patt 68 (71: 74: 77: 80: 83) sts and turn, leaving rem sts on a holder.

Work each side of neck separately.

Work 7 rows, ending with RS facing for next row.

Shape armhole
Keeping patt correct, bind off 8 (8: 9: 9: 10: 10) sts at beg of next row. 60 (63: 65: 68: 70: 73) sts.

Work 1 row.

Dec 1 st at armhole edge of next 5 (7: 7: 9: 9: 11) rows, then on foll 3 (3: 4: 4: 5: 5) alt rows, then on 2 foll 4th rows. 50 (51: 52: 53: 54: 55) sts.

Work even until 21 rows fewer have been worked than on Back to start of shoulder shaping, ending with WS facing for next row.

Shape neck
Keeping patt correct, bind off 11 (11: 11: 12: 12: 12) sts at beg of next row. 39 (40: 41: 41: 42: 43) sts.

Dec 1 st at neck edge of next 5 rows, then on foll 5 alt rows, then on foll 4th row. 28 (29: 30: 30: 31: 32) sts.

Work 1 row, ending with RS facing for next row.

Shape shoulder
Bind off 9 (10: 10: 10: 10: 11) sts at beg of next row and foll alt row.

Work 1 row.

Bind off rem 10 (9: 10: 10: 11: 10) sts.

With RS facing, rejoin yarn to rem sts, patt to end.

Complete to match first side, reversing shapings.

SLEEVES (make 2)
Using size 3 (3.25mm) needles, cast on 57 (57: 59: 61: 61: 63) sts.

Row 1 (RS) K0 (0: 1: 2: 2: 3), P3, *K3, P3; rep from * to last 0 (0: 1: 2: 2: 3) sts, K0 (0: 1: 2: 2: 3).

Row 2 P0 (0: 1: 2: 2: 3), K3, *P3, K3; rep from * to last 0 (0: 1: 2: 2: 3) sts, P0 (0: 1: 2: 2: 3).

These 2 rows form rib.

Work in rib for 13 rows more, ending with WS facing for next row.

Row 16 (WS) Rib 19 (19: 20: 21: 21: 22), [M1, rib 3] twice, [M1, rib 2] 4 times, [M1, rib 3] twice, M1, rib to last st, inc in last st. 67 (67: 69: 71: 71: 73) sts.

Change to size 6 (4mm) needles.

Now work in cable patt as follows:

Row 1 (RS) P0 (0: 1: 0: 0: 1), [K1, P1] 9 (9: 9: 10: 10: 10) times, [P1, K1 tbl] twice, P3, K1 tbl, P1, K1 tbl, P2, K7, P2, K1 tbl, P1, K1 tbl, P3, [K1 tbl, P1] twice, [P1, K1] 9 (9: 9: 10: 10: 10) times, P0 (0: 1: 0: 0: 1).

Row 2 P0 (0: 1: 0: 0: 1), [K1, P1] 9 (9: 9: 10: 10: 10) times, [K1, P1 tbl] twice, K3, P1 tbl, K1, P1 tbl, K2, P7, K2, P1 tbl, K1, P1 tbl, K3, [P1 tbl, K1] twice, [P1, K1] 9 (9: 9: 10: 10: 10) times, P0 (0: 1: 0: 0: 1).

These 2 rows set position of seed st at sides of central cable panel.

Keeping seed st correct as now set, cont as follows:

Row 3 Seed st 18 (18: 19: 20: 20: 21) sts, [P1, K1 tbl] twice, P3, K1 tbl, P1, K1 tbl, P2, C3B, K1, C3F, P2, K1 tbl, P1, K1 tbl, P3, [K1 tbl, P1] twice, seed st to end.

Row 4 Rep row 2.

Row 5 Seed st 18 (18: 19: 20: 20: 21) sts, P1, K1 tbl, P1, Tw2L, P1, Tw2R, P1, K1 tbl, P2, K7, P2, K1 tbl, P1, Tw2L, P1, Tw2R, P1, K1 tbl, P1, seed st to end.

Row 6 Seed st 18 (18: 19: 20: 20: 21) sts, K1, P1 tbl, K2, P1 tbl, K1, [P1 tbl, K2] twice, P7, [K2, P1 tbl] twice, K1, P1 tbl, K2, P1 tbl, K1, seed st to end.

Row 7 Seed st 18 (18: 19: 20: 20: 21) sts, P1, K1 tbl, P2, Cr3L, P2, K1 tbl, P2, C3B, K1, C3F, P2, K1 tbl, P2, Cr3L, P2, K1 tbl, P1, seed st to end.

Row 8 Rep row 6.

Row 9 [Inc in first st] 0 (0: 0: 0: 1: 1) times, seed st 18 (18: 19: 20: 19: 20) sts, P1, K1 tbl, P1, Tw2R, P1, Tw2L, P1, K1 tbl, P2, K7, P2, K1 tbl, P1, Tw2R, P1, Tw2L, P1, K1 tbl, P1, seed st to last 0 (0: 0: 0: 1: 1) st, [inc in last st] 0 (0: 0: 0: 1: 1) times. 67 (67: 69: 71: 73: 75) sts.

Row 10 Seed st 18 (18: 19: 20: 21: 22) sts, [K1, P1 tbl] twice, K3, P1 tbl, K1, P1 tbl, K2, P7, K2, P1 tbl, K1, P1 tbl, K3, [P1 tbl, K1] twice, seed st to end.

Row 11 [Inc in first st] 0 (1: 1: 1: 0: 0) times, seed st 18 (17: 18: 19: 21: 22) sts, [P1, K1 tbl] twice, P3, K1 tbl, P1, K1 tbl, P2, C3B, K1, C3F, P2, K1 tbl, P1, K1 tbl, P3, [K1 tbl, P1] twice, seed st to last 0 (1: 1: 1: 0: 0) st, [inc in last st] 0 (1: 1: 1: 0: 0) times. 67 (69: 71: 73: 73: 75) sts.

Row 12 Seed st 18 (19: 20: 21: 21: 22) sts, [K1, P1 tbl] twice, K3, P1 tbl, K1, P1 tbl, K2, P7, K2, P1 tbl, K1, P1 tbl, K3, [P1 tbl, K1] twice, seed st to end.

These 12 rows form patt and start sleeve shaping (for largest 5 sizes).

Cont in patt, shaping sides by inc 1 st at each end of next (11th: 11th: 11th: 9th: 9th) row and every foll

14th (12th: 12th: 12th: 12th: 12th) row until there are 81 (79: 77: 79: 91: 93) sts, taking inc sts into seed st.

38, 40, 42, and 44in sizes only

Inc 1 st at each end of every foll 16th (14th: 14th: 14th) row until there are 83 (85: 87: 89) sts.

All sizes

Work even until Sleeve measures 20¼ (20¼: 20½: 20½: 20½: 20½)in/51.5 (51.5: 52.5: 52.5: 52.5: 52.5)cm from cast-on edge, ending with RS facing for next row.

Shape top of sleeve

Keeping patt correct, bind off 8 (8: 9: 9: 10: 10) sts at beg of next 2 rows. 67 (69: 69: 71: 71: 73) sts.

Dec 1 st at each end of next 5 rows, then on foll 3 alt rows, then on every foll 4th row until 37 (39: 39: 41: 41: 43) sts rem.

Work 1 row.

Dec 1 st at each end of next row and every foll alt row until 29 sts rem, then on foll 3 rows, ending with RS facing for next row.

Bind off rem 23 sts.

HOOD

Using size 6 (4mm) needles, cast on 85 (85: 85: 89: 89: 89) sts.

Work in seed st as given for Back for 2 rows, ending with RS facing for next row.

Place marker on center st of last row.

Row 3 (RS) Seed st to marked st, M1, seed st marked st, M1, seed st to end.

Working all increases as set by last row, inc 1 st at each side of marked center back st on 4th row and every foll 4th row until there are 97 (97: 97: 101: 101: 101) sts, taking inc sts into seed st.

Work even until Hood measures 14½in/37cm from cast-on edge, ending with RS facing for next row.

Next row (RS) Seed st to within 2 sts of marked st, work 2 tog tbl, seed st marked st, work 2 tog, seed st to end.

Working all decreases as set by last row, dec 1 st at each side of marked center back st on 4th row and every foll alt row until 87 (87: 87: 91: 91: 91) sts rem, ending with WS facing for next row.

Next row (WS) Seed st to within 1 st of marked st, work 2 tog (marked st is 2nd of these 2 sts), seed st to end. 86 (86: 86: 90: 90: 90) sts.

Next row Seed st 43 (43: 43: 45: 45: 45) sts and turn.

Fold Hood in half with RS facing each other and, using a spare needle, bind off both sets of 43 (43: 43: 45: 45: 45) sts together by taking one st from one needle with correspond st from other needle (to form top seam of Hood).

FINISHING

Do NOT press.

Sew shoulder seams. Sew sleeves into armholes. Sew side and sleeve seams, leaving side seams open for first 46 rows.

Hood border

With RS facing and using size 3 (3.25mm) circular needle, pick up and knit 153 sts evenly along straight row-end edge of Hood.

Row 1 (WS) K3, *P3, K3; rep from * to end.

Row 2 P3, *K3, P3; rep from * to end.

These 2 rows form rib.

Work in rib for 6 rows more, ending with WS facing for next row.

Bind off in rib (on WS).

Matching bound-off edge of Hood Border to front opening edges and easing in Hood to fit, sew cast-on edge of Hood to neck edge.

Pocket tops (both alike)

Slip 37 sts left on pocket holder onto size 3 (3.25mm) needles and rejoin yarn with RS facing.

Row 1 (RS) P2, K3, *P3, K3; rep from * to last 2 sts, P2.

Row 2 K2, P3, *K3, P3; rep from * to last 2 sts, K2.

These 2 rows form rib.

Work in rib for 6 rows more, ending with WS facing for next row.

Bind off in rib (on WS).

Sew Pocket Linings in place on inside, then neatly sew down ends of Pocket Tops.

Make 4 twisted cords, each 11in/28cm long, and knot one end, leaving a little tassel of approximately ³⁄₄in/2cm. Attach other ends of twisted cords to front opening edges—position top pair of cords just below neck seam, and second pair of cords approximately 3¹⁄₄in/8cm up from base of front opening.

Hot machine wash completed garment and tumble dry (to shrink to correct length).

ribbed shawl

MARTIN STOREY

TO FIT BUST

38–40	42–44	46–48	in
97–102	107–112	117–122	cm

FINISHED MEASUREMENTS

Width of sections

13¼	14½	15¼	in
34	37	39	cm

Total length, around entire lower edge

60½	66	69¼	in
154	168	176	cm

YARN

12 (14: 15) x 1¾oz/109yd balls of Rowan Classic *Silk Wool DK* in Clay 305

NEEDLES

Pair of size 6 (4mm) knitting needles

GAUGE

32 sts and 30 rows to 4in/10cm measured over rib using size 6 (4mm) needles *or size to obtain correct gauge.*

ABBREVIATIONS

See page 132.

LEFT SECTION

Using size 6 (4mm) needles, cast on 110 (118: 126) sts.
Row 1 (RS) K2, *P2, K2; rep from * to end.
Row 2 P2, *K2, P2; rep from * to end.
These 2 rows form rib.
Work in rib until Left Section measures 13¼ (14½: 15¼)in/ 34 (37: 39)cm from cast-on edge, ending with RS facing for next row.

Place marker at beg of last row.
Work 4 rows, ending with RS facing for next row.
Shape for collar
Next row (RS) Rib to last 34 sts and turn, leaving rem 34 sts on a holder (for Collar).
Cast on 34 sts at beg of next row.
Work even until work measures 17 (18½: 19¼)in/43 (47: 49)cm from marker, ending with RS facing for next row.
Break off yarn and leave sts on a holder.

RIGHT SECTION

Using size 6 (4mm) needles, cast on 110 (118: 126) sts.
Work in rib as given for Left Section for 4 rows, ending with RS facing for next row.
Shape for collar
Next row (RS) Rib 34 sts and slip these sts onto a holder (for Collar), cast on 34 sts, rib to end.
Work even until Right Section measures 17 (18½: 19¼)in/ 43 (47: 49)cm from cast-on edge, ending with RS facing for next row.
Join sections
Holding Left and Right Sections with RS together, bind off sts from both sections together by taking one st from one Section with correspond st from other Section (to form center back seam).

FINISHING

Do NOT press.
Left collar
Slip 34 sts on Left Section holder onto size 6 (4mm), rejoin yarn with RS facing, and rib to end.
Work in rib as set, shaping collar by inc 1 st at end of 2nd row and foll alt row, then on every foll 4th row until

there are 48 sts, taking inc sts into rib.

Work even until Collar, unstretched, fits up row-end edge of Left Section to center back seam, ending with RS facing for next row.

Break off yarn and leave sts on a holder.

Right collar

Slip 34 sts on Right Section holder onto size 6 (4mm), rejoin yarn with WS facing, and rib to end.

Work in rib as set, shaping collar by inc 1 st at beg of next row and foll alt row, then on every foll 4th row until there are 48 sts, taking inc sts into rib.

Work even until Collar, unstretched, fits up row-end edge of Right Section to center back seam, ending with RS facing for next row.

Join collars

Holding Left and Right Collars with RS together, bind off sts from both sections together by taking one st from one Section with correspond st from other Section (to form center back seam).

Sew cast-on edge of Right Section to row-end edge of Left Section from cast-on edge to marker. Sew shaped row-end edges of collars to row-end edges of Left and Right Sections, matching center back seams.

seed stitch jacket

WENDY BAKER

TO FIT BUST

38	40	42	44	46	48	in
97	102	107	112	117	122	cm

FINISHED MEASUREMENTS

Around bust

47½	49¼	51½	53	55½	57	in
121	125	131	135	141	145	cm

Length to shoulder

28¼	28¾	29	29½	30	30¼	in
72	73	74	75	76	77	cm

Sleeve seam

17¾	17¾	18	18	18	18	in
45	45	46	46	46	46	cm

YARN

17 (18: 19: 20: 21: 21) x 1¾oz/123yd balls of Rowan *Scottish Tweed DK* in Indigo 031

NEEDLES

Pair of size 6 (4mm) knitting needles

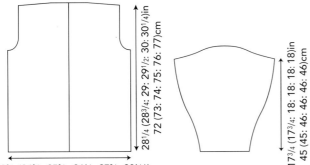

23¾ (24¾: 25¾: 26½: 27¾: 28½)in
60.5 (62.5: 65.5: 67.5: 70.5: 72.5)cm

28¼ (28¾: 29: 29½: 30: 30¼)in
72 (73: 74: 75: 76: 77)cm

17¾ (17¾: 18: 18: 18: 18)in
45 (45: 46: 46: 46: 46)cm

EXTRAS

1 large decorative pin (or kilt pin) for fastening (optional)

SPECIAL NOTE

If you like, you can make a shorter felted version of this jacket using exactly the same pattern. Once the garment is completed, machine wash it to shrink and felt it, then dry it flat. The amount the garment will shrink will depend on how hot it is washed, but, roughly, you will need to knit a garment two sizes larger than you would normally, to ensure that it will still fit once shrunk and felted.

GAUGE

20 sts and 32 rows to 4in/10cm measured over seed st using size 6 (4mm) needles *or size to obtain correct gauge.*

ABBREVIATIONS

See page 132.

BACK

Using size 6 (4mm) needles, cast on 121 (125: 131: 135: 141: 145) sts.

Row 1 (RS) K1, *P1, K1; rep from * to end.

Row 2 Rep row 1.

These 2 rows form seed st.

Work in seed st until Back measures 19½ (19½: 20: 20: 20½: 20½)in/50 (50: 51: 51: 52: 52)cm from cast-on edge, ending with RS facing for next row.

Shape armholes

Keeping seed st correct, bind off 3 sts at beg of next 2 rows. 115 (119: 125: 129: 135: 139) sts.

Dec 1 st at each end of next row and 2 foll 4th rows.

109 (113: 119: 123: 129: 133) sts.

Work even until armhole measures 8½ (9: 9: 9½: 9½: 9¾)in/22 (23: 23: 24: 24: 25)cm, ending with RS facing for next row.

Shape shoulders

Bind off 10 (11: 12: 12: 13: 14) sts at beg of next 4 rows, then 11 (11: 12: 13: 14: 14) sts at beg of foll 2 rows.
Bind off rem 47 (47: 47: 49: 49: 49) sts.

LEFT FRONT

Using size 6 (4mm) needles, cast on 85 (87: 90: 92: 95: 97) sts.

Row 1 (RS) *K1, P1; rep from * to last 1 (1: 0: 0: 1: 1) st, K1 (1: 0: 0: 1: 1).

Row 2 K1 (1: 0: 0: 1: 1), *P1, K1; rep from * to end.
These 2 rows form seed st.
Work in seed st until Left Front matches Back to start of armhole shaping, ending with RS facing for next row.

Shape armhole

Keeping seed st correct, bind off 3 sts at beg of next row. 82 (84: 87: 89: 92: 94) sts.

Work 1 row.

Dec 1 st at armhole edge of next row and 2 foll 4th rows. 79 (81: 84: 86: 89: 91) sts.

Work even until Left Front matches Back to start of shoulder shaping, ending with RS facing for next row.

Shape shoulder

Bind off 10 (11: 12: 12: 13: 14) sts at beg of next row and foll alt row, then 11 (11: 12: 13: 14: 14) sts at beg of foll alt row.

Work 1 row, ending with RS facing for next row.
Break off yarn and leave rem 48 (48: 48: 49: 49: 49) sts on a holder.

RIGHT FRONT

Using size 6 (4mm) needles, cast on 85 (87: 90:

92: 95: 97) sts.

Row 1 (RS) K1 (1: 0: 0: 1: 1), *P1, K1; rep from * to end.

Row 2 *K1, P1; rep from * to last 1 (1: 0: 0: 1: 1) st, K1 (1: 0: 0: 1: 1).

These 2 rows form seed st.

Work in seed st until Right Front matches Back to start of armhole shaping, ending with WS facing for next row.

Shape armhole

Keeping seed st correct, bind off 3 sts at beg of next row. 82 (84: 87: 89: 92: 94) sts.

Dec 1 st at armhole edge of next row and 2 foll 4th rows. 79 (81: 84: 86: 89: 91) sts.

Work even until Right Front matches Back to start of shoulder shaping, ending with WS facing for next row.

Shape shoulder

Bind off 10 (11: 12: 12: 13: 14) sts at beg of next row and foll alt row, then 11 (11: 12: 13: 14: 14) sts at beg of foll alt row, ending with RS facing for next row.

Leave rem 48 (48: 48: 49: 49: 49) sts on a holder and do NOT break off yarn but set aside this ball of yarn to use for Collar.

SLEEVES (make 2)

Using size 6 (4mm) needles, cast on 55 (55: 57: 59: 59: 61) sts.

Work in seed st as given for Back for 2in/5cm, ending with RS facing for next row.

Inc 1 st at each end of next row and every foll 6th (4th: 6th: 4th: 4th: 4th) row to 89 (65: 95: 65: 65: 73) sts, then on every foll 8th (6th: 8th: 6th: 6th: 6th) row until there are 93 (97: 97: 101: 101: 105) sts, taking inc sts into seed st.

Work even until Sleeve measures 17¾ (17¾: 18: 18: 18: 18)in/45 (45: 46: 46: 46: 46)cm from cast-on edge, ending with RS facing for next row.

Shape top of sleeve

Keeping seed st correct, bind off 3 sts at beg of next

6 rows, then 6 sts at beg of foll 8 rows.
Bind off rem 27 (31: 31: 35: 35: 39) sts.

FINISHING

Press lightly on WS following instructions on yarn label.
Sew shoulder seams.

Collar

With RS facing, using size 6 (4mm) needles and ball of
yarn set aside with Right Front, seed st across 48 (48: 48:
49: 49: 49) sts on right front holder, pick up and knit
47 (47: 47: 49: 49: 49) sts from back, then seed st across
48 (48: 48: 49: 49: 49) sts on left front holder. 143 (143:
143: 147: 147: 147) sts.
Work in seed st as set by Front sts until Collar measures
5cm/2in from pick-up row, ending with RS facing for
next row.
Bind off in seed st.
Sew sleeves into armholes. Sew side and sleeve seams.
Fasten fronts with a decorative pin if desired.

SEED STITCH JACKET

large collar jacket

MARTIN STOREY

TO FIT BUST						
38	40	42	44	46	48	in
97	102	107	112	117	122	cm
FINISHED MEASUREMENTS						
Around bust						
44	46	48½	50½	52¼	54¼	in
112	117	123	128	133	138	cm
Length to back neck						
23¼	23½	24	24½	24¾	25	in
59	60	61	62	63	64	cm
Sleeve seam						
17	17	17¼	17¼	17¼	17¼	in
43	43	44	44	44	44	cm

YARN

12 (13: 13: 14: 15: 15) x 1¾oz/123yd balls of Rowan
Scottish Tweed DK in Celtic Mix 022

NEEDLES

Pair of size 5 (3.75mm) knitting needles

22 (23: 24¼: 25¼: 26¼: 27¼)in
56 (58.5: 61.5: 64: 66.5: 69)cm

23¼ (23½: 24: 24½: 24¾: 25)in
59 (60: 61: 62: 63: 64)cm

17 (17: 17¼: 17¼: 17¼: 17¼)in
43 (43: 44: 44: 44: 44)cm

EXTRAS

1 large button

GAUGE

23 sts and 31 rows to 4in/10cm measured over patt using size 5 (3.75mm) needles *or size to obtain correct gauge.*

ABBREVIATIONS

See page 132.

BACK

Using size 5 (3.75mm) needles, cast on 129 (135: 141: 147: 153: 159) sts.

Row 1 (RS) K1 (0: 1: 0: 1: 0), *P1, K1; rep from * to last 0 (1: 0: 1: 0: 1) st, P0 (1: 0: 1: 0: 1).

Rows 2 and 3 P1 (0: 1: 0: 1: 0), *K1, P1; rep from * to last 0 (1: 0: 1: 0: 1) st, K0 (1: 0: 1: 0: 1).

Row 4 Rep row 1.

These 4 rows form patt.

Work in patt for 16 rows more, ending with RS facing for next row.

Keeping patt correct, dec 1 st at each end of next row and 2 foll 8th rows, then on 3 foll 6th rows. 117 (123: 129: 135: 141: 147) sts.

Work 7 rows, ending with RS facing for next row.

Inc 1 st at each end of next row and every foll 8th row until there are 129 (135: 141: 147: 153: 159) sts, taking inc sts into patt.

Work even until Back measures 14½ (14½: 15: 15: 15¼: 15¼)in/37 (37: 38: 38: 39: 39)cm from cast-on edge, ending with RS facing for next row.

Shape armholes

Keeping patt correct, bind off 7 (8: 8: 9: 9: 10) sts at beg of next 2 rows. 115 (119: 125: 129: 135: 139) sts.

Dec 1 st at each end of next 5 (5: 7: 7: 9: 9) rows, then on foll 3 (4: 4: 5: 5: 6) alt rows, then on 2 foll 4th rows. 95 (97: 99: 101: 103: 105) sts.

Work even until armhole measures 8½ (9: 9: 9½: 9½: 9¾)in/22 (23: 23: 24: 24: 25)cm, ending with RS facing for next row.

Shape back neck and shoulders

Bind off 9 (9: 10: 10: 10: 10) sts at beg of next 2 rows. 77 (79: 79: 81: 83: 85) sts.

Next row (RS) Bind off 9 (9: 10: 10: 10: 10) sts, patt until there are 13 (14: 13: 13: 14: 15) sts on right needle and turn, leaving rem sts on a holder.

Work each side of neck separately.

Bind off 4 sts at beg of next row.

Bind off rem 9 (10: 9: 9: 10: 11) sts.

With RS facing, rejoin yarn to rem sts, bind off center 33 (33: 33: 35: 35: 35) sts, patt to end.

Complete this side of neck to match first side, reversing shapings.

LEFT FRONT

Using size 5 (3.75mm) needles, cast on 65 (68: 71: 74: 77: 80) sts.

Row 1 (RS) K1 (0: 1: 0: 1: 0), *P1, K1; rep from * to end.

Row 2 *P1, K1; rep from * to last 1 (0: 1: 0: 1: 0) st, P1 (0: 1: 0: 1: 0).

Row 3 P1 (0: 1: 0: 1: 0), *K1, P1; rep from * to end.

Row 4 *K1, P1; rep from * to last 1 (0: 1: 0: 1: 0) st, K1 (0: 1: 0: 1: 0).

These 4 rows form patt.

Work in patt for 16 rows more, ending with RS facing for next row.

Keeping patt correct, dec 1 st at beg of next row and 2 foll 8th rows, then on 3 foll 6th rows. 59 (62: 65: 68: 71: 74) sts.

Work 7 rows, ending with RS facing for next row.

Inc 1 st at beg of next row and every foll 8th row until there are 65 (68: 71: 74: 77: 80) sts, taking inc sts into patt.

Work even until Left Front matches Back to start of armhole shaping, ending with RS facing for next row.

Shape armhole and front slope

Keeping patt correct, bind off 7 (8: 8: 9: 9: 10) sts at beg and dec 1 st at end of next row. 57 (59: 62: 64: 67: 69) sts. Work 1 row.

Dec 1 st at armhole edge of next 5 (5: 7: 7: 9: 9) rows, then on foll 3 (4: 4: 5: 5: 6) alt rows, then on 2 foll 4th rows **and at the same time** dec 1 st at front slope edge of next row and foll 9 (8: 8: 9: 9: 7) alt rows, then on 0 (1: 1: 1: 2: 3) foll 4th rows. 37 (38: 39: 39: 39: 41) sts.

Dec 1 st at front slope edge only on 2nd (4th: 2nd: 2nd: 4th: 2nd) row and every foll 4th row until 27 (28: 29: 29: 30: 31) sts rem.

Work even until Left Front matches Back to start of shoulder shaping, ending with RS facing for next row.

Shape shoulder

Bind off 9 (9: 10: 10: 10: 10) sts at beg of next row and foll alt row.

Work 1 row.

Bind off rem 9 (10: 9: 9: 10: 11) sts.

RIGHT FRONT

Using size 5 (3.75mm) needles, cast on 65 (68: 71: 74: 77: 80) sts.

Row 1 (RS) [K1, P1] twice, wrap next st (by slipping next st from left needle onto right needle, taking yarn to opposite side of work between needles and then slipping same st back onto left needle) and turn.

Row 2 [K1, P1] twice.

Row 3 [P1, K1] 4 times, wrap next st and turn.

Row 4 [P1, K1] 4 times.

These 4 rows form patt and start front hem edge shaping.

Keeping patt correct as now set, work as follows:

Row 5 Patt 12 sts, wrap next st and turn.

Row 6 Patt to end.

Row 7 Patt 16 sts, wrap next st and turn.

Row 8 Patt to end.

Row 9 Patt 20 sts, wrap next st and turn.

Row 10 Patt to end.

Cont in this way, working 4 more sts on next row and every foll alt row before wrapping next st and turning, until the foll row has been worked:

Next row (RS) Patt 60 (64: 64: 68: 72: 76) sts, wrap next st and turn.

Next row Patt to end.

Now working in patt across all sts, work as follows:

Work 19 rows, ending with RS facing for next row.

Keeping patt correct, dec 1 st at end of next row and 2 foll 8th rows, then on 3 foll 6th rows. 59 (62: 65: 68: 71: 74) sts.

Work 7 rows, ending with RS facing for next row.

Inc 1 st at end of next row and every foll 8th row until there are 65 (68: 71: 74: 77: 80) sts, taking inc sts into patt.

Work even until 2 rows fewer have been worked than on Back to start of armhole shaping, measuring at side seam edge and ending with RS facing for next row.

Next row (buttonhole row) (RS) Patt 6 sts, bind off 3 sts (to make buttonhole), patt to end.

Next row Patt to end, casting on 3 sts over those bound off on previous row.

Shape armhole and front slope

Keeping patt correct, dec 1 st at beg of next row then bind off 7 (8: 8: 9: 9: 10) sts at beg of foll row. 57 (59: 62: 64: 67: 69) sts.

Complete to match Left Front, reversing shapings.

SLEEVES (make 2)

Using size 5 (3.75mm) needles, cast on 79 (79: 81: 83: 83: 85) sts.

Row 1 (RS) K1, *P1, K1; rep from * to end.

Rows 2 and 3 P1, *K1, P1; rep from * to end.

Row 4 Rep row 1.

These 4 rows form patt.

Work in patt for 12 rows more, ending with RS facing for next row.

Inc 1 st at each end of next row and every foll 20th (16th: 16th: 16th: 14th: 14th) row to 89 (87: 87: 89: 93: 95) sts, then on every foll 22nd (18th: 18th: 18th: 16th: 16th) row until there are 91 (93: 95: 97: 99: 101) sts, taking inc sts into patt.

Work even until Sleeve measures 17 (17: 17¼: 17¼: 17¼: 17¼)in/43 (43: 44: 44: 44: 44)cm from cast-on edge, ending with RS facing for next row.

Shape top of sleeve

Keeping patt correct, bind off 7 (8: 8: 9: 9: 10) sts at beg of next 2 rows. 77 (77: 79: 79: 81: 81) sts.

Dec 1 st at each end of next 5 rows, then on foll 8 alt rows, then on every foll 4th row until 47 (47: 49: 49: 51: 51) sts rem.

Work 1 row.

Dec 1 st at each end of next row and every foll alt row until 33 sts rem, then on foll 5 rows, ending with RS facing for next row.
Bind off rem 23 sts.

FINISHING

Press lightly on WS following instructions on yarn label.
Sew shoulder seams.

Collar

Using size 5 (3.75mm) needles, cast on 161 (169: 169: 175: 175: 183) sts.
Work in patt as given for Sleeves for 9in/23cm, ending with RS facing for next row.
Keeping patt correct, bind off 12 (12: 12: 13: 13: 14) sts at beg of next 10 (2: 2: 8: 8: 10) rows, then 0 (13: 13: 14: 14: 0) sts at beg of foll 0 (8: 8: 2: 2: 0) rows.
Bind off rem 41 (41: 41: 43: 43: 43) sts.
Sew sleeves into armholes. Sew side and sleeve seams. Sew shaped bound-off edge of collar to front slope and back neck edges, positioning row-ends of collar at start of front slope shaping and making sure that the RS of collar is facing when collar is turned over.
Sew on button.

collared tunic

KIM HARGREAVES

TO FIT BUST						
38	40	42	44	46	48	in
97	102	107	112	117	122	cm
FINISHED MEASUREMENTS						
Around bust						
46	48½	50½	52¼	54¼	56¼	in
117	123	128	133	138	143	cm
Length to back neck						
27	27½	28	28¼	28¾	29	in
69	70	71	72	73	74	cm
Sleeve seam						
16	16	16½	16½	16½	16½	in
41	41	42	42	42	42	cm

YARN

14 (14: 15: 16: 16: 17) x 1¾oz/126yd balls of Rowan *Cotton Glace* in Oyster 730

NEEDLES

Pair of size 2 (2.75mm) knitting needles
Pair of size 3 (3.25mm) knitting needles

EXTRAS

9 buttons

GAUGE

23 sts and 32 rows to 4in/10cm measured over St st using size 3 (3.25mm) needles *or size to obtain correct gauge.*

ABBREVIATIONS

See page 132.

SPECIAL ABBREVIATION

M2 = make 2 sts by picking up, onto left needle, horizontal loop between needles and working [K1, P1] into back of this loop.

BACK

Using size 2 (2.75mm) needles, cast on 135 (141: 147: 153: 159: 165) sts.

Row 1 (RS) K1, *P1, K1; rep from * to end.

Row 2 Rep row 1.

These 2 rows form seed st.

Work in seed st until Back measures 3in/8cm, ending with RS facing for next row.

Change to size 3 (3.25mm) needles.

Starting with a K row, work in St st until Back measures 18 (18: 18½: 18½: 18½: 19)in/46 (46: 47: 47: 47: 48)cm from cast-on edge, ending with RS facing for next row.

Shape raglan armholes

Bind off 7 (6: 7: 7: 6: 7) sts at beg of next 2 rows.

121 (129: 133: 139: 147: 151) sts.

Next row (RS) K2, K3tog, K to last 5 sts, K3tog tbl, K2.

Working all raglan decreases as set by last row, dec 2 sts

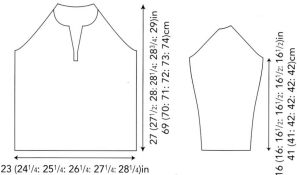

27 (27½: 28: 28¼: 28¾: 29)in
69 (70: 71: 72: 73: 74)cm

16 (16: 16½: 16½: 16½: 16½)in
41 (41: 42: 42: 42: 42)cm

23 (24¼: 25¼: 26¼: 27¼: 28¼)in
58.5 (61.5: 64: 66.5: 69: 71.5)cm

at each end of 2nd row and foll 5 (8: 9: 10: 13: 14) alt rows, then on every foll 4th row until 37 (37: 37: 39: 39: 39) sts rem.

Work 3 rows, ending with RS facing for next row.

Bind off.

FRONT

Work as given for Back until 32 rows fewer have been worked than on Back to start of raglan armhole shaping, ending with RS facing for next row.

Divide for front opening

Next row (RS) K65 (68: 71: 74: 77: 80) and turn, leaving rem sts on a holder.

Work each side of neck separately.

Work 23 rows, ending with RS facing for next row.

Next row K to last 4 sts, K2tog, K2. 64 (67: 70: 73: 76: 79) sts.

Working all front opening edges as set by last row, work as follows:

Work 7 rows, ending with RS facing for next row.

Shape raglan armhole

Bind off 7 (6: 7: 7: 6: 7) sts at beg and dec 1 (1: 1: 0: 0: 0) st at end of next row. 56 (60: 62: 66: 70: 72) sts.

Work 1 row.

Keeping front opening edge decreases correct as set and working all raglan armhole decreases in same way as for back raglan armholes, dec 2 sts at raglan armhole edge of next row and foll 6 (9: 10: 11: 14: 15) alt rows, then on 9 (8: 8: 8: 7: 7) foll 4th rows, ending with WS facing for next row, **and at the same time** dec 1 st at front opening edge of 7th (7th: 7th: next: next: next) row and 4 (4: 4: 5: 5: 5) foll 8th (8th: 8th: 10th: 10th: 10th) rows. 19 (19: 19: 20: 20: 20) sts.

Shape neck

Bind off 4 (4: 4: 5: 5: 5) sts at beg of next row. 15 sts.

Dec 1 st at neck edge of next row and foll 4 alt rows **and at the same time** dec 2 sts at raglan armhole edge of 3rd and foll 4th row. 6 sts.

Work 1 row.

Next row (RS) K2, K4tog tbl.

Next row P3.

Next row K1, K2tog.

Next row P2.

Next row K2tog and fasten off.

With RS facing, rejoin yarn to rem sts, bind off center

5 sts, K to end. 65 (68: 71: 74: 77: 80) sts.

Work 23 rows, ending with RS facing for next row.

Next row K2, K2tog tbl, K to end. 64 (67: 70: 73: 76: 79) sts.

Working all front opening edges as set by last row, complete to match first side, reversing shapings.

LEFT SLEEVE

Front cuff

Using size 2 (2.75mm) needles, cast on 37 (37: 37: 39: 39: 39) sts.

Work in seed st as given for Back for 4 rows, ending with RS facing for next row.

Row 5 (RS) Seed st 3 sts, [yo] twice (to make a buttonhole, drop extra loop on next row), work 2 tog, seed st to end.

Work 11 rows.

Rep last 12 rows once more, then row 5 again.

Work 3 rows, ending with RS facing for next row.

Change to size 3 (3.25mm) needles.

Row 33 (RS) Knit.

Row 34 P to last st, K1.

These 2 rows set the sts.

Row 35 K to last 2 sts, M1, K2.

Keeping sts correct and working all increases as set by last row, work 11 rows, inc 1 st at end of 6th of these rows. 39 (39: 39: 41: 41: 41) sts.

Break off yarn and leave sts on a holder.

Back cuff

Using size 2 (2.75mm) needles, cast on 17 (17: 19: 19: 19: 21) sts.

Work in seed st as given for Back for 32 rows, ending with RS facing for next row.

Change to size 3 (3.25mm) needles.

Row 33 (RS) Knit.

Row 34 K1, P to end.

These 2 rows set the sts.

Row 35 K2, M1, K to end.

Keeping sts correct and working all increases as set by last row, work 11 rows, inc 1 st at beg of 6th of these rows. 19 (19: 21: 21: 21: 23) sts.

Join cuffs

Next row (RS) Across sts of Back Cuff work [K2, M1, K to last st], now holding WS of Front Cuff against RS of Back Cuff, K tog first st of Front Cuff with last st of Back Cuff,

across rem sts of Front Cuff work
[K to last 2 sts, M1, K2]. 59 (59: 61:
63: 63: 65) sts.

Working all increases as set and
starting with a P row, work in St st,
shaping sides by inc 1 st at each end
of 6th row and every foll 6th row to
73 (81: 79: 81: 89: 91) sts, then on
every foll 8th row until there are
83 (85: 87: 89: 91: 93) sts.

Work even until Sleeve measures
16 (16: 16½: 16½: 16½: 16½)in/
41 (41: 42: 42: 42: 42)cm from
cast-on edge, ending with RS facing
for next row.

Shape raglan

Bind off 7 (6: 7: 7: 6: 7) sts at beg of
next 2 rows. 69 (73: 73: 75: 79: 79) sts.

Next row (RS) K2, K2tog, K to last
4 sts, K2tog tbl, K2.

Working all raglan decreases as set
by last row, dec 1 st at each end of
4th row and 7 (6: 7: 7: 6: 7) foll 4th
rows, then on every foll alt row until
19 sts rem, ending with WS facing
for next row.

Shape neck

Bind off 3 sts at beg of next row.
16 sts.

Dec 1 st at beg of next row, then
bind off 4 sts at beg of foll row. 11 sts.
Rep last 2 rows once more. 6 sts.
Dec 1 st at beg of next row, then
bind off 3 sts at beg of foll row.
2 sts.

Next row (RS) K2tog and fasten off.

RIGHT SLEEVE
Back cuff

Using size 2 (2.75mm) needles, cast
on 17 (17: 19: 19: 19: 21) sts.
Work in seed st as given for Back for
32 rows, ending with RS facing for
next row.
Change to size 3 (3.25mm) needles.

Row 33 (RS) Knit.

Row 34 P to last st, K1.

These 2 rows set the sts.

Row 35 K to last 2 sts, M1, K2.

Keeping sts correct and working all increases as set by last row, work 11 rows, inc 1 st at end of 6th of these rows. 19 (19: 21: 21: 21: 23) sts.

Break off yarn and leave sts on a holder.

Front cuff

Using size 2 (2.75mm) needles, cast on 37 (37: 37: 39: 39: 39) sts.

Work in seed st as given for Back for 4 rows, ending with RS facing for next row.

Row 5 (RS) Seed st to last 5 sts, work 2 tog, [yo] twice (to make a buttonhole, drop extra loop on next row), seed st 3 sts.

Work 11 rows.

Rep last 12 rows once more, then row 5 again.

Work 3 rows, ending with RS facing for next row.

Change to size 3 (3.25mm) needles.

Row 33 (RS) Knit.

Row 34 K1, P to end.

These 2 rows set the sts.

Row 35 K2, M1, K to end.

Keeping sts correct and working all increases as set by last row, work 11 rows, inc 1 st at beg of 6th of these rows. 39 (39: 39: 41: 41: 41) sts.

Join cuffs

Next row (RS) Across sts of Front Cuff work [K2, M1, K to last st], now holding WS of Front Cuff against RS of Back Cuff, K tog last st of Front Cuff with first st of Back Cuff, across rem sts of Back Cuff work [K to last 2 sts, M1, K2]. 59 (59: 61: 63: 63: 65) sts.

Working all increases as set and starting with a P row, work in St st, shaping sides by inc 1 st at each end of 6th row and every foll 6th row to 73 (81: 79: 81: 89: 91) sts, then on every foll 8th row until there are 83 (85: 87: 89: 91: 93) sts.

Work even until Sleeve measures 16 (16: 16½: 16½: 16½: 16½)in/41 (41: 42: 42: 42: 42)cm from cast-on edge, ending with RS facing for next row.

Shape raglan

Bind off 7 (6: 7: 7: 6: 7) sts at beg of next 2 rows. 69 (73: 73: 75: 79: 79) sts.

Next row (RS) K2, K2tog, K to last 4 sts, K2tog tbl, K2. Working all raglan decreases as set by last row, dec 1 st at each end of 4th row and 7 (6: 7: 7: 6: 7) foll 4th rows, then on every foll alt row until 21 sts rem, ending with RS facing for next row.

Shape neck
Bind off 4 sts at beg and dec 1 st at end of next row. 16 sts.
Work 1 row.
Rep last 2 rows twice more. 6 sts.
Bind off 4 sts at beg of next row. 2 sts.
Work 1 row.
Next row (RS) K2tog and fasten off.

FINISHING
Press lightly on WS following instructions on yarn label.
Sew raglan seams.

Button band
Using size 2 (2.75mm) needles, cast on 7 sts.
Work in seed st as given for Back until Button Band, when slightly stretched, fits up left front opening edge, from base of front opening to start of neck shaping, sewing in place as you go along and ending with RS facing for next row. Break off yarn and leave sts on a holder.
Mark positions for 3 buttons on this Band—first to come 5/8in/1.5cm up from base of opening, last to come level with first dec along front opening edge, and rem button spaced evenly between.

Buttonhole band
Using size 2 (2.75mm) needles, cast on 7 sts.
Work in seed st as given for Back until Buttonhole Band, when slightly stretched, fits up right front opening edge, from base of front opening to start of neck shaping, sewing in place as you go along, ending with RS facing for next row and with the addition of 3 buttonholes worked to correspond with positions marked for buttons on Button Band as follows:
Buttonhole row (RS) Seed st 3 sts, [yo] twice (to make a buttonhole, drop extra loop on next row), work 2 tog, seed st 2 sts.
When Band is complete, do NOT break off yarn.

Collar
With RS facing and using size 2 (2.75mm) needles, seed st 7 sts of Buttonhole Band, pick up and knit 17 (17: 17: 18: 18: 18) sts up right side of neck, 16 sts from top

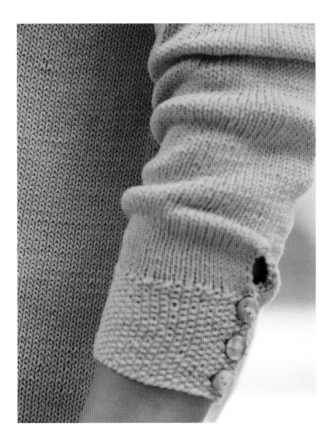

of Right Sleeve, 37 (37: 37: 39: 39: 39) sts from Back, 16 sts from top of Left Sleeve, and 17 (17: 17: 18: 18: 18) sts down left side of neck, then seed st across 7 sts left on Button Band holder. 117 (117: 117: 121: 121: 121) sts.
Keeping seed st correct as set by Band sts, work in seed st for 3 rows, ending with RS of Body (WS of Collar) facing for next row.
Next row Seed st 2 sts, M2, seed st to last 2 sts, M2, seed st 2 sts.
Work 3 rows.
Rep last 4 rows 6 times more. 145 (145: 145: 149: 149: 149) sts.
Bind off in seed st.
Sew side and sleeve seams. Lay Buttonhole Band over Button Band and sew cast-on edges of Bands to bound-off edge at base of front opening. Sew buttons to neck opening and cuffs.

bow sweater

WENDY BAKER

TO FIT BUST						
38	40	42	44	46	48	in
97	102	107	112	117	122	cm
FINISHED MEASUREMENTS						
Around bust						
41¾	43¾	45½	47½	49½	51½	in
106	111	116	121	126	131	cm
Length to back neck						
24	24	24½	24½	24¾	24¾	in
61	61	62	62	63	63	cm
Sleeve seam						
13¾	13¾	14	14	14	14	in
35	35	36	36	36	36	cm

YARN

8 (9: 9: 10: 10: 10) x 1¾oz/197yd balls of Rowan Classic *Cashsoft 4-Ply* in Loganberry 430

NEEDLES

Pair of size 2 (3mm) knitting needles
Pair of size 3 (3.25mm) knitting needles

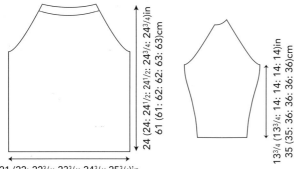

21 (22: 22¾: 23¾: 24¾: 25¾)in
53 (55.5: 58: 60.5: 63: 65.5)cm

24 (24: 24½: 24½: 24¾: 24¾)in
61 (61: 62: 62: 63: 63)cm

13¾ (13¾: 14: 14: 14: 14)in
35 (35: 36: 36: 36: 36)cm

GAUGE

28 sts and 36 rows to 4in/10cm measured over St st using size 3 (3.25mm) needles *or size to obtain correct gauge.*

ABBREVIATIONS

See page 132.

BACK

Using size 2 (3mm) needles, cast on 149 (155: 163: 169: 177: 183) sts.

Row 1 (RS) K1, *P1, K1; rep from * to end.

Row 2 Rep row 1.

These 2 rows form seed st.

Work in seed st for 16 rows more, ending with RS facing for next row.

Change to size 3 (3.25mm) needles.**

Starting with a K row, work in St st until Back measures 7¾in/20cm from cast-on edge, ending with RS facing for next row.

Change to size 2 (3mm) needles.

Work even until Back measures 10¼in/26cm from cast-on edge, ending with RS facing for next row.

Change to size 3 (3.25mm) needles.

Work even until Back measures 15¾in/40cm from cast-on edge, ending with RS facing for next row.

Shape raglan armholes

Bind off 7 sts at beg of next 2 rows. 135 (141: 149: 155: 163: 169) sts.

Next row (RS) K2, sl 1, K1, psso, K to last 4 sts, K2tog, K2.

Next row [P2, P2tog] 0 (0: 0: 0: 0: 1) times, P to last 0 (0: 0: 0: 0: 4) sts, [P2tog tbl, P2] 0 (0: 0: 0: 0: 1) times.

Working all raglan armhole decreases as set by last 2 rows, cont as follows:

Work 2 (2: 2: 2: 0: 0) rows.

Dec 1 st at each end of next 1 (1: 1: 1: 1: 3) rows, then on 8 (6: 3: 2: 0: 0) foll 4th rows, then on every foll alt row until 107 (107: 107: 109: 109: 109) sts rem.

Work 1 row, ending with RS facing for next row.

Shape back neck

Next row (RS) K2, sl 1, K1, psso, K14, K2tog, K2 and turn, leaving rem sts on a holder. 20 sts.

Work each side of neck separately.

Working all neck decreases in same way as raglan armhole decreases, dec 1 st at each end of 2nd row and foll 5 alt rows. 8 sts.

Dec 1 st at raglan armhole edge only on 2nd row and foll 4 alt rows. 3 sts.

Next row (WS) P3.

Next row K1, sl 1, K1, psso.

Next row P2.

Next row K2tog and fasten off.

With RS facing, rejoin yarn to rem sts, bind off center 63 (63: 63: 65: 65: 65) sts, K2, sl 1, K1, psso, K to last 4 sts, K2tog, K2. 20 sts.

Working all neck decreases in same way as raglan armhole decreases, dec 1 st at each end of 2nd row and foll 5 alt rows. 8 sts.

Dec 1 st at raglan armhole edge only on 2nd row and foll 4 alt rows. 3 sts.

Next row (WS) P3.

Next row K2tog, K1.

Next row P2.

Next row K2tog and fasten off.

FRONT

Work as given for Back to **.

Next row (RS) K39 (41: 44: 46: 49: 51), yo, K1, sl 1, K2tog, psso, K1, yo, K61 (63: 65: 67: 69: 71), yo, K1, sl 1, K2tog, psso, K1, yo, K to end.

Next row Purl.

Rep last 2 rows until Front measures 7¾in/20cm from cast-on edge, ending with RS facing for next row.

Change to size 2 (3mm) needles.

Starting with a K row, work in St st until Front measures 10¼in/26cm from cast-on edge, ending with RS facing for next row.

Change to size 3 (3.25mm) needles.

Work even until Front matches Back to start of raglan armhole shaping, ending with RS facing for next row.

Shape raglan armholes

Bind off 7 sts at beg of next 2 rows. 135 (141: 149: 155: 163: 169) sts.

Working all raglan armhole decreases as set by Back, dec 1 st at each end of next 1 (1: 1: 1: 1: 5) rows, then on 5 (6: 4: 3: 0: 0) foll 4th rows, then on foll 0 (0: 5: 8: 15: 14) alt rows. 123 (127: 129: 131: 131: 131) sts.

Work 3 (1: 1: 1: 1: 1) rows, ending with RS facing for next row.

Shape front neck

Next row (RS) [K2, sl 1, K1, psso] 1 (0: 1: 1: 1: 1) times, K33 (39: 36: 36: 36: 36), K2tog, K2 and turn, leaving rem sts on a holder. 39 (42: 42: 42: 42: 42) sts.

Work each side of neck separately.

Working all neck decreases in same way as raglan armhole decreases, dec 1 st at neck edge of 2nd row and foll 17 alt rows **and at the same time** dec 1 st at raglan armhole edge of 4th (2nd: 2nd: 2nd: 2nd: 2nd) row and 2 (0: 0: 0: 0: 0) foll 4th rows, then on foll 12 (17: 17: 17: 17: 17) alt rows. 6 sts.

Next row (WS) P6.

Next row K2, sl 1, K2tog, psso, K1.

Next row P4.

Next row K1, sl 1, K2tog, psso.

Next row P2.

Next row K2tog and fasten off.

With RS facing, rejoin yarn to rem sts, bind off center 41 (41: 41: 43: 43: 43) sts, K2, sl 1, K1, psso, K to last 4 (0: 4: 4: 4: 4) sts, [K2tog, K2] 1 (0: 1: 1: 1: 1) times. 39 (42: 42: 42: 42: 42) sts.

Working all neck decreases in same way as raglan armhole decreases, dec 1 st at neck edge of 2nd row and foll 17 alt rows **and at the same time** dec 1 st at raglan armhole edge of 4th (2nd: 2nd: 2nd: 2nd: 2nd) row and 2 (0: 0: 0: 0: 0) foll 4th rows, then on foll 12 (17: 17: 17: 17: 17) alt rows. 6 sts.

Next row (WS) P6.

Next row K1, K3tog, K2.

Next row P4.

Next row K3tog, K1.

Next row P2.

Next row K2tog and fasten off.

KNITTING GOES LARGE

SLEEVES (make 2)

Using size 2 (3mm) needles, cast on 73 (73: 75: 77: 77: 79) sts.

Work in seed st as given for Back for 18 rows, ending with RS facing for next row.

Change to size 3 (3.25mm) needles.

Next row (RS) K34 (34: 35: 36: 36: 37), yo, K1, sl 1, K2tog, psso, K1, yo, K to end.

Next row Purl.

These 2 rows form patt.

Next row K4, M1, patt to last 4 sts, M1, K4.

Working all sleeve increases as set by last row, inc 1 st at each end of 4th row and 4 (6: 5: 5: 6: 6) foll 4th rows, then on 1 (0: 0: 0: 0: 0) foll 6th row. 87 (89: 89: 91: 93: 95) sts.

Work in patt for 3 (1: 5: 5: 1: 1) rows more, ending with RS facing for next row.

Starting with a K row, work in St st, inc 1 st at each end of 3rd (3rd: next: next: 3rd: 3rd) row and 0 (0: 0: 0: 1: 1) foll 4th row, then on every foll 6th row until there are 109 (111: 113: 115: 117: 119) sts.

Work even until Sleeve measures 13¾ (13¾: 14: 14: 14: 14)in/35 (35: 36: 36: 36: 36)cm from cast-on edge, ending with RS facing for next row.

Shape raglan

Bind off 7 sts at beg of next 2 rows. 95 (97: 99: 101: 103: 105) sts.

Working all raglan decreases in same way as for raglan armholes, dec 1 st at each end of next row and every foll alt row until 29 sts rem.

Work 1 row.

Left sleeve only

Dec 1 st at each end of next row, then bind off 6 sts at beg of foll row. 21 sts.

Dec 1 st at beg of next row, then bind off 6 sts at beg of foll row. 14 sts.

Right sleeve only

Bind off 7 sts at beg and dec 1 st at end of next row. 21 sts.

Work 1 row.

Bind off 6 sts at beg and dec 1 st at end of next row. 14 sts.

Work 1 row.

Both sleeves

Rep last 2 rows once more.

Bind off rem 7 sts.

FINISHING

Press lightly on WS following instructions on yarn label. Sew both front and right back raglan seams.

Neckband

With RS facing and using size 3 (3.25mm) needles, pick up and knit 21 sts from top of left sleeve, 31 sts down left side of neck, 41 sts from front, 31 sts up right side of neck, 21 sts from top of right sleeve, 16 sts down right side of back neck, 63 sts from back, then 16 sts up left side of back neck. 240 sts.

Row 1 (WS) *K1, P1; rep from * to end.

Row 2 *P1, K1; rep from * to end.

These 2 rows form seed st.

Work in seed st for 5 rows more, ending with RS facing for next row.

Row 8 (RS) *Seed st 7 sts, work 3 tog; rep from * to end. 192 sts.

Change to size 2 (3mm) needles.

Work in seed st for 5 rows, ending with RS facing for next row.

Row 14 (RS) *Seed st 13 sts, work 3 tog; rep from * to end. 168 sts.

Work in seed st for 3 rows, ending with RS facing for next row.

Bind off in seed st.

Sew left back raglan and Neckband seam. Sew side and sleeve seams.

Bow

Using size 2 (3mm) needles, cast on 21 sts.

Work in seed st as given for Back, inc 1 st at each end of 2nd row and foll 4 alt rows. 31 sts.

Work 3 rows, ending with WS facing for next row.

Dec 1 st at each end of next row and foll 4 alt rows, ending with RS facing for next row.

Bind off rem 21 sts in seed st.

Bow Center

Using size 2 (3mm) needles, cast on 5 sts.

Work in seed st as given for Back for 23 rows, ending with WS facing for next row.

Bind off in seed st (on WS).

Sew together cast-on and bound-off ends of Bow Center to form a loop. Slip Bow through Bow Center and attach to Neckband as shown.

split neck tunic

KIM HARGREAVES

TO FIT BUST						
38	40	42	44	46	48	in
97	102	107	112	117	122	cm
FINISHED MEASUREMENTS						
Around bust						
50¼	52¼	54¼	56¼	58½	60½	in
128	133	138	143	149	154	cm
Length to shoulder						
29	29½	30	30¼	30¾	31	in
74	75	76	77	78	79	cm
Sleeve seam						
18	18	18½	18½	18½	18½	in
46	46	47	47	47	47	cm

YARN

16 (17: 18: 19: 19: 20) x 1¾oz/126yd balls of Rowan
Cotton Glace in Sky 749

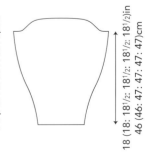

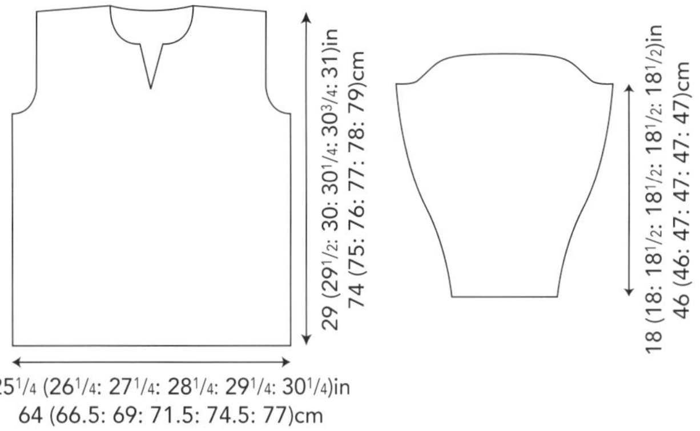

29 (29½: 30: 30¼: 30¾: 31)in
74 (75: 76: 77: 78: 79)cm

18 (18: 18½: 18½: 18½: 18½)in
46 (46: 47: 47: 47: 47)cm

25¼ (26¼: 27¼: 28¼: 29¼: 30¼)in
64 (66.5: 69: 71.5: 74.5: 77)cm

NEEDLES

Pair of size 2 (2.75mm) knitting needles

Pair of size 3 (3.25mm) knitting needles

GAUGE

23 sts and 32 rows to 4in/10cm measured over St st using size 3 (3.25mm) needles *or size to obtain correct gauge.*

ABBREVIATIONS

See page 132.

BACK

Using size 2 (2.75mm) needles, cast on 147 (153: 159: 165: 171: 177) sts.

Row 1 (RS) K1, *P1, K1; rep from * to end.

Row 2 Rep row 1.

These 2 rows form seed st.

Work in seed st for 16 rows more, ending with RS facing for next row.

Change to size 3 (3.25mm) needles.

Row 19 (RS) Seed st 11 sts, K to last 11 sts, seed st 11 sts.

Row 20 Seed st 11 sts, P to last 11 sts, seed st 11 sts.

Rep these 2 rows until Back measures 11¾in/30cm from cast-on edge, ending with RS facing for next row.

Starting with a K row, work in St st until Back measures 19¼ (19¼: 19½: 19½: 20: 20)in/49 (49: 50: 50: 51: 51)cm from cast-on edge, ending with RS facing for next row.

Shape armholes

Bind off 4 sts at beg of next 2 rows. 139 (145: 151: 157: 163: 169) sts.

Next row (RS) K3, K3tog, K to last 6 sts, K3tog tbl, K3.

Next row Purl.

Rep last 2 rows 6 times more. 111 (117: 123: 129: 135: 141) sts.

Work even until armhole measures 9¾ (10¼: 10¼: 10½: 10½: 11)in/25 (26: 26: 27: 27: 28)cm, ending with RS facing for next row.

Shape back neck and shoulders

Bind off 8 (9: 10: 11: 12: 13) sts at beg of next 2 rows. 95 (99: 103: 107: 111: 115) sts.

Next row (RS) Bind off 8 (9: 10: 11: 12: 13) sts, K until there are 13 (14: 15: 16: 17: 18) sts on right needle and turn, leaving rem sts on a holder.

Work each side of neck separately.

Bind off 4 sts at beg of next row.

Bind off rem 9 (10: 11: 12: 13: 14) sts.

With RS facing, rejoin yarn to rem sts, bind off center 53 sts, K to end.

Complete to match first side, reversing shapings.

FRONT

Lower right front

Using size 2 (2.75mm) needles, cast on 74 (77: 80: 83: 86: 89) sts.

Row 1 (RS) K0 (1: 0: 1: 0: 1), *P1, K1; rep from * to end.

Row 2 *K1, P1; rep from * to last 0 (1: 0: 1: 0: 1) st, K0 (1: 0: 1: 0: 1).

These 2 rows form seed st.

Work in seed st for 16 rows more, ending with RS facing for next row.

Change to size 3 (3.25mm) needles.

Row 19 (RS) Seed st 9 sts, K to last 11 sts, seed st 11 sts.

Row 20 Seed st 11 sts, P to last 9 sts, seed st 9 sts.

Rep these 2 rows until Lower Right Front measures 6in/15cm from cast-on edge, ending with RS facing for next row.

Break off yarn and leave sts on a holder.

Lower left front

Using size 2 (2.75mm) needles, cast on 74 (77: 80: 83: 86: 89) sts.

Row 1 (RS) *K1, P1; rep from * to last 0 (1: 0: 1: 0: 1) st, K0 (1: 0: 1: 0: 1).

Row 2 K0 (1: 0: 1: 0: 1), *P1, K1; rep from * to end.

These 2 rows form seed st.

Work in seed st for 16 rows more, ending with RS facing for next row.

Change to size 3 (3.25mm) needles.

Row 19 (RS) Seed st 11 sts, K to last 9 sts, seed st 9 sts.

Row 20 Seed st 9 sts, P to last 11 sts, seed st 11 sts.

Rep these 2 rows until Lower Left Front measures 6in/15cm from cast-on edge, ending with RS facing for next row.

Join sections

Next row (RS) Patt first 73 (76: 79: 82: 85: 88) sts of Lower Left Front, work tog last st of Lower Left Front with first st of Lower Right Front, patt to end. 146 (152: 158: 164: 170: 176) sts.

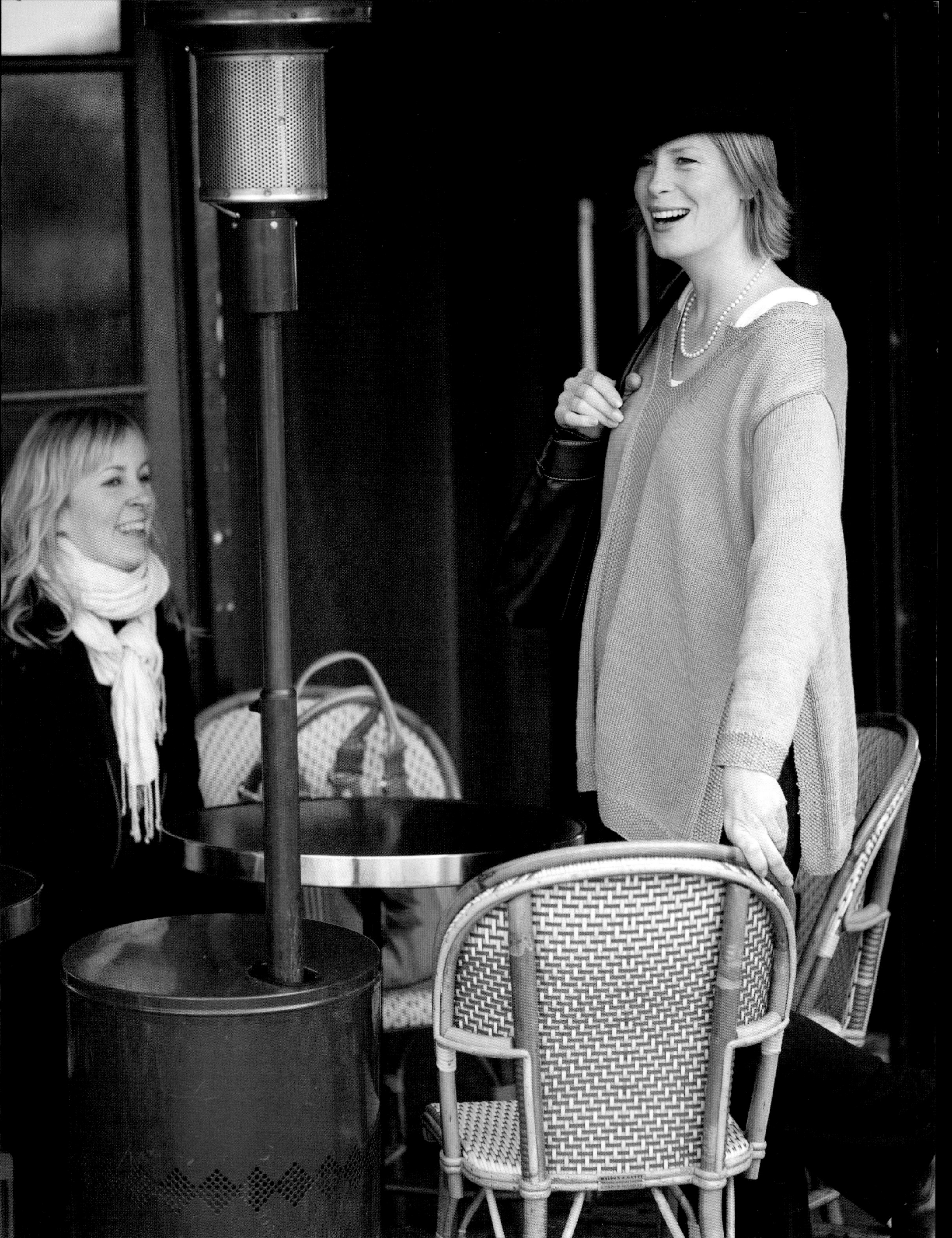

Keeping sts correct as set, work even until Front measures 11¾in/30cm from cast-on edge, ending with RS facing for next row.

Next row (RS) K65 (68: 71: 74: 77: 80), seed st 17 sts, K to end.

Next row P65 (68: 71: 74: 77: 80), seed st 17 sts, P to end.

Last 2 rows set the sts for rest of Front—center 17 sts in seed st with all other sts in St st.

Keeping sts correct as set, work even until Front matches Back to start of armhole shaping, ending with RS facing for next row.

Shape armholes

Keeping sts correct, bind off 4 sts at beg of next 2 rows. 139 (145: 151: 157: 163: 169) sts.

Next row (RS) K3, K3tog, patt to last 6 sts, K3tog tbl, K3.

Next row Patt.

Rep last 2 rows 6 times more. 111 (117: 123: 129: 135: 141) sts.

Work 2 rows, ending with RS facing for next row.

Divide for front opening

Next row (RS) K41 (44: 47: 50: 53: 56), K3tog, K3, seed st 8 sts and turn, leaving rem sts on a holder. 53 (56: 59: 62: 65: 68) sts.

Work each side of neck separately.

Keeping sts correct, work 9 (11: 11: 11: 11: 13) rows, ending with RS facing for next row.

Next row K to last 14 sts, K3tog, K3, seed st 8 sts.

Rep last 10 (12: 12: 12: 12: 14) rows once more. 49 (52: 55: 58: 61: 64) sts.

Work even until 34 rows fewer have been worked than on Back to start of shoulder shaping, ending with RS facing for next row.

Shape neck

Next row (RS) K to last 14 sts, K3tog, K3 and turn, leaving rem 8 sts on a holder. 39 (42: 45: 48: 51: 54) sts.

Working all neck decreases in same way as for armhole and front opening decreases, dec 2 sts at neck edge of 2nd and foll alt row, then on 5 foll 4th rows. 25 (28: 31: 34: 37: 40) sts.

Work 9 rows, ending with RS facing for next row.

Shape shoulder

Bind off 8 (9: 10: 11: 12: 13) sts at beg of next row and foll alt row.

Work 1 row.

Bind off rem 9 (10: 11: 12: 13: 14) sts.

With RS facing, at front opening divide rejoin yarn to rem sts, work 2 tog, seed st 7 sts, K3, K3tog tbl, K to end.

Complete to match first side, reversing shapings and working first row of neck shaping as follows:

Shape neck

Next row (RS) Seed st 8 sts and slip these sts onto a holder, K3, K3tog tbl, K to end. 39 (42: 45: 48: 51: 54) sts.

SLEEVES (make 2)

Using size 2 (2.75mm) needles, cast on 55 (55: 57: 59: 59: 61) sts.

Work in seed st as given for Back for 18 rows, ending with RS facing for next row.

Change to size 3 (3.25mm) needles.

Next row (RS) K3, M1, K to last 3 sts, M1, K3.

Working all increases as set by last row and starting with a P row, work in St st, shaping sides by inc 1 st at each end of 2nd and foll 1 (5: 2: 4: 4: 6) alt rows, then on every foll 4th row until there are 115 (119: 119: 123: 123: 127) sts.

Work even until Sleeve measures 18 (18: 18½: 18½: 18½: 18½)in/46 (46: 47: 47: 47: 47)cm from cast-on edge, ending with RS facing for next row.

Shape top of sleeve

Bind off 4 sts at beg of next 2 rows. 107 (111: 111: 115: 115: 119) sts.

Working all decreases in same way as given for armhole decreases, dec 2 sts at each end of next row and foll 5 alt rows.

Work 1 row.

Bind off rem 83 (87: 87: 91: 91: 95) sts.

FINISHING

Press lightly on WS following instructions on yarn label. Sew shoulder seams.

Neckband

Slip 8 sts from right front holder onto size 2 (2.75mm) needles, rejoin yarn with RS facing and pick up and knit 25 sts up right side of neck, 61 sts from back, and 25 sts down left side of neck, then seed st across 8 sts left on left front holder. 127 sts.

Work in seed st as set by first and last 8 sts for 9 rows, ending with RS facing for next row.

Bind off in rib.

Matching shaped edges at underarm and center of sleeve bound-off edge to shoulder seam, sew sleeves into armholes. Sew side and sleeve seams, leaving side seams open for first 11¾in/30cm.

cabled vest

WENDY BAKER

TO FIT BUST

38	40	42	44	46	48	in
97	102	107	112	117	122	cm

FINISHED MEASUREMENTS

Around bust

42	44½	46½	49	50¾	53	in
107	113	118	124	129	135	cm

Length to shoulder

34¼	34½	35	35½	35¾	36¼	in
87	88	89	90	91	92	cm

YARN

12 (13: 13: 14: 15: 15) x 1¾oz/123yd balls of Rowan *Wool Cotton* in Misty 903

NEEDLES

Pair of size 3 (3.25mm) knitting needles
Pair of size 6 (4mm) knitting needles
Size 3 (3.25mm) circular knitting needle
Cable needle

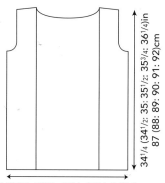

21 (22¼: 23¼: 24½: 25½: 26½)in
53.5 (56.5: 59: 62: 64.5: 67.5)cm

34¼ (34½: 35: 35½: 35¾: 36¼)in
87 (88: 89: 90: 91: 92)cm

EXTRAS

1 large decorative pin (or kilt pin) for fastening (optional)

GAUGE

22 sts and 30 rows to 4in/10cm measured over rev St st using size 6 (4mm) needles *or size to obtain correct gauge.*

ABBREVIATIONS

See page 132.

SPECIAL ABBREVIATIONS

Cr3R = slip next st onto cable needle and leave at back of work, K2, then P1 from cable needle; **Cr3L** = slip next 2 sts onto cable needle and leave at front of work, P1, then K2 from cable needle; **C4B** = slip next 2 sts onto cable needle and leave at back of work, K2, then K2 from cable needle; **C4F** = slip next 2 sts onto cable needle and leave at front of work, K2, then K2 from cable needle.

SPECIAL NOTE

When working cable panel from chart, read panel odd-numbered (RS) rows from right to left, and even-numbered (WS) rows from left to right.

BACK

Using size 6 (4mm) needles, cast on 18 sts.
Row 1 (RS) Work across these 18 sts as row 21 of Cable Panel (see chart on page 58).
Row 2 Cast on and K 4 (5: 6: 7: 8: 9) sts, work next 18 sts as row 22 of Cable Panel.
Row 3 Cast on and P 4 (5: 6: 7: 8: 9) sts, work next 18 sts as row 23 of Cable Panel, P to end.

CABLE PANEL

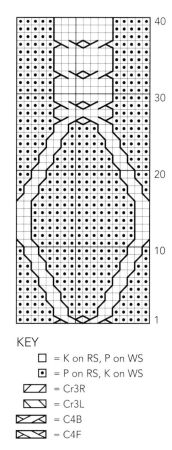

KEY

☐ = K on RS, P on WS

⊡ = P on RS, K on WS

◩ = Cr3R

◪ = Cr3L

▨ = C4B

▧ = C4F

These 3 rows set position of Cable Panel with rev St st at sides.

Keeping patt correct, work as follows:

Row 4 Cast on and K 4 (5: 6: 7: 8: 9) sts, patt to end.

Row 5 Cast on and P 4 (5: 6: 7: 8: 9) sts, patt to end.

Row 6 Cast on 9 sts and work [K4, P2, K3] across these 9 sts, patt to end.

Row 7 Cast on 9 sts and work [P4, Cr3L, P2] across these 9 sts, patt to last 9 sts, P2, Cr3R, P4.

Row 8 Cast on 9 sts and work [K2, P2, K5] across these 9 sts, then K5, P2, K2, patt to last 9 sts, K2, P2, K5.

Row 9 Cast on 9 sts and work [P1, Cr3R, P5] across these 9 sts, then P5, Cr3L, P1, patt to last 18 sts, work last 18 sts as row 9 of Cable Panel.

Row 10 Cast on and K 4 (5: 6: 7: 8: 9) sts, work next 18 sts as row 10 of Cable Panel, patt to last 18 sts, work last 18 sts as row 10 of Cable Panel.

Last 2 rows set position of 3 Cable Panels with rev St st between and at sides.

Keeping patt correct, work as follows:

Row 11 Cast on and P 4 (5: 6: 7: 8: 9) sts, patt to end.

Row 12 Cast on and K 4 (5: 6: 7: 8: 9) sts, patt to end.

Row 13 Cast on and P 4 (5: 6: 7: 8: 9) sts, patt to end.

Row 14 Cast on 9 sts and work [P4, K5] across these 9 sts, patt to end.

Row 15 Cast on 9 sts and work [K4, P5] across these 9 sts, patt to last 9 sts, P5, K4.

Row 16 Cast on 9 sts and work [K5, P4] across these 9 sts, then P4, K5, patt to last 9 sts, K5, P4.

Row 17 Cast on 9 sts and work [P5, C4B] across these 9 sts, then C4F, P5, patt to last 18 sts, work last 18 sts as row 37 of Cable Panel.

Row 18 Cast on and K 4 (5: 6: 7: 8: 9) sts, work next 18 sts as row 38 of Cable Panel, patt to last 18 sts, work last 18 sts as row 38 of Cable Panel.

Last 2 rows set position of 5 Cable Panels with rev St st between and at sides.

Keeping patt correct, work as follows:

Row 19 Cast on and P 4 (5: 6: 7: 8: 9) sts, patt to end.

Row 20 Cast on and K 4 (5: 6: 7: 8: 9) sts, patt to end.

Row 21 Cast on and P 4 (5: 6: 7: 8: 9) sts, patt to end. 138 (144: 150: 156: 162: 168) sts.

Keeping patt correct, work even until Back measures 19½ (19½: 20: 20: 20½: 20½)in/50 (50: 51: 51: 52: 52)cm from original center cast-on edge, ending

with RS facing for next row.

Keeping patt correct, bind off 4 sts at beg of next 2 rows. 130 (136: 142: 148: 154: 160) sts.

Dec 1 st at each end of next row and 2 foll 4th rows. 124 (130: 136: 142: 148: 154) sts.

Work even until armhole measures 6½ (7: 7: 7½: 7½: 7¾)in/17 (18: 18: 19: 19: 20)cm, ending with RS facing for next row.

Next row (RS) Patt 36 (39: 42: 44: 47: 50) sts and turn, leaving rem sts on a holder.

Work each side of neck separately.

Keeping patt correct, dec 1 st at neck edge of next row and foll 9 alt rows, ending with RS facing for next row. 26 (29: 32: 34: 37: 40) sts.

Bind off 13 (14: 16: 17: 18: 20) sts at beg of next row. Work 1 row.

Bind off rem 13 (15: 16: 17: 19: 20) sts.

With RS facing, rejoin yarn to rem sts, bind off center 52 (52: 52: 54: 54: 54) sts, patt to end.

Complete to match first side, reversing shapings.

LEFT FRONT

Using size 6 (4mm) needles, cast on 4 (5: 6: 7: 8: 9) sts.

Row 1 (RS) Purl.

Row 2 Cast on and K 4 (5: 6: 7: 8: 9) sts, K to end.

Row 3 Purl.

Row 4 Cast on 9 sts and work [K3, P2, K4] across these 9 sts, then K to end.

Row 5 P12 (14: 16: 18: 20: 22), P4, Cr3L, P2.

Row 6 Cast on 9 sts and work [K5, P2, K2] across these 9 sts, then K2, P2, K to end.

Row 7 P8 (10: 12: 14: 16: 18), work last 18 sts as row 27 of Cable Panel.

Row 8 Cast on and K 4 (5: 6: 7: 8: 9) sts, work next 18 sts as row 28 of Cable Panel, K to end.

Last 2 rows set position of Cable Panel with rev St st at sides.

Keeping patt correct, work as follows:

Row 9 Patt to end.

Row 10 Cast on and K 3 (3: 3: 2: 2: 2) sts, patt to end. 33 (36: 39: 41: 44: 47) sts.

Keeping patt correct, work even until side seam (longer)

edge of Left Front matches side seam edge of Back to start of armhole shaping, ending with RS facing for next row.

Shape armhole

Keeping patt correct, bind off 4 sts at beg of next row.
29 (32: 35: 37: 40: 43) sts.

Work 1 row.

Dec 1 st at armhole edge of next row and 2 foll 4th rows.
26 (29: 32: 34: 37: 40) sts.

Work even until Left Front matches Back to start of shoulder shaping, ending with RS facing for next row.

Shape shoulder

Bind off 13 (14: 16: 17: 18: 20) sts at beg of next row.

Work 1 row.

Bind off rem 13 (15: 16: 17: 19: 20) sts.

RIGHT FRONT

Using size 6 (4mm) needles, cast on 4 (5: 6: 7: 8: 9) sts.

Row 1 (RS) Purl.

Row 2 Knit.

Row 3 Cast on and P 4 (5: 6: 7: 8: 9) sts, P to end.

Row 4 Knit.

Row 5 Cast on 9 sts and work [P2, Cr3R, P4] across these 9 sts, then P to end.

Row 6 K13 (15: 17: 19: 21: 23), P2, K2.

Row 7 Cast on 9 sts and work [P5, C4F] across these 9 sts, then C4B, P to end.

Row 8 K8 (10: 12: 14: 16: 18), work last 18 sts as row 28 of Cable Panel.

Row 9 Cast on and P 4 (5: 6: 7: 8: 9) sts, work next 18 sts as row 29 of Cable Panel, P to end.

Row 10 K8 (10: 12: 14: 16: 18), work next 18 sts as row 30 of Cable Panel, K to end.

Last 2 rows set position of Cable Panel with rev St st at sides.

Keeping patt correct, work as follows:

Row 11 Cast on and P 3 (3: 3: 2: 2: 2) sts, patt to end.
33 (36: 39: 41: 44: 47) sts.

Keeping patt correct, complete to match Left Front, reversing shapings.

FINISHING

Press lightly on WS following instructions on yarn label.
Sew shoulder seams.

Armhole borders (both alike)

With RS facing and using size 3 (3.25mm) needles, pick up and knit 118 (122: 122: 126: 126: 130) sts evenly all around armhole edge.

Row 1 (WS) P2, *K2, P2; rep from * to end.

Row 2 K2, *P2, K2; rep from * to end.

These 2 rows form rib.

Work in rib for 9 rows more, ending with RS facing for next row.

Bind off in rib.

Sew side and Armhole Border seams.

Hem border

With RS facing and using size 3 (3.25mm) needles, starting and ending at base of straight front opening row-end edges, pick up and knit 35 (38: 41: 44: 47: 50) sts along shaped cast-on edge of left front, 128 (134: 140: 146: 152: 158) sts along shaped cast-on edge of back, then 35 (38: 41: 44: 47: 50) sts along shaped cast-on edge of right front. 198 (210: 222: 234: 246: 258) sts.

Starting with row 1, work in rib as given for Armhole Borders for 43 rows, ending with RS facing for next row.

Bind off in rib.

Front border

With RS facing and using size 3 (3.25mm) circular needle, starting and ending at bound-off edge of Hem Border, pick up and knit 176 (182: 186: 191: 195: 199) sts up entire right front opening edge, 18 sts down right side of back neck, 46 (46: 46: 48: 48: 48) sts from back, 18 sts up left side of back neck, then 176 (182: 186: 191: 195: 199) sts down entire left front opening edge. 434 (446: 454: 466: 474: 482) sts.

Starting with row 1, work in rib as given for Armhole Borders for 43 rows, ending with RS facing for next row.

Bind off in rib.

Fasten fronts with decorative pin if desired.

fair isle sweater

WENDY BAKER

TO FIT BUST						
38	40	42	44	46	48	in
97	102	107	112	117	122	cm
FINISHED MEASUREMENTS						
Around bust						
45½	47¼	49½	51	53½	55	in
116	120	126	130	136	140	cm
Length to back neck						
26¾	26¾	27	27	27½	28	in
68	68	69	69	70	71	cm
Sleeve seam						
17	17	17¼	17¼	17¼	17¼	in
43	43	44	44	44	44	cm

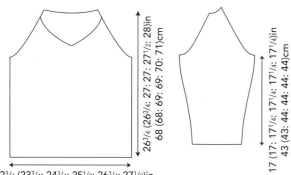

26¾ (26¾: 27: 27: 27½: 28)in
68 (68: 69: 69: 70: 71)cm

22¾ (23¾: 24¾: 25½: 26¾: 27½)in
58 (60: 63: 65: 68: 70)cm

17 (17: 17¼: 17¼: 17¼: 17¼)in
43 (43: 44: 44: 44: 44)cm

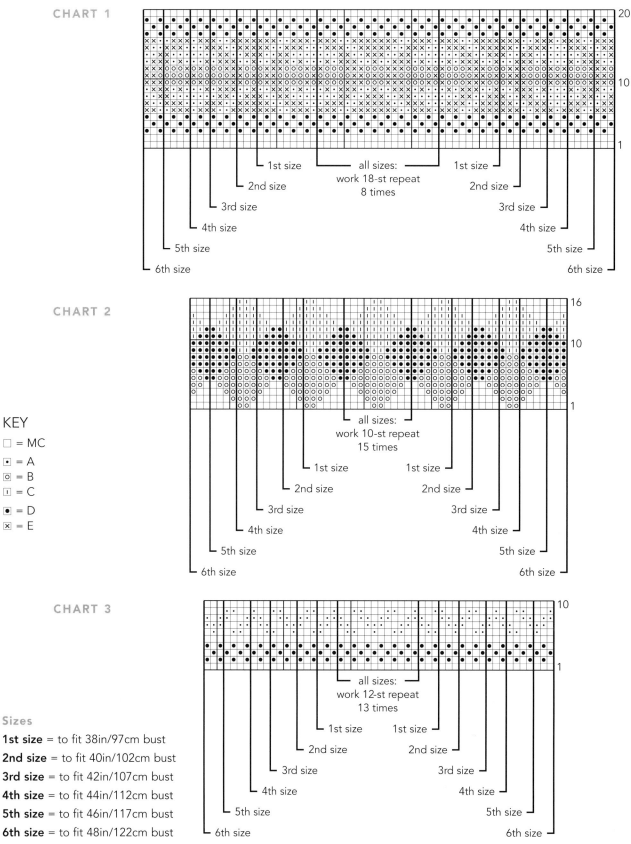

CHART 1

20

10

1

1st size
all sizes:
work 18-st repeat
8 times
1st size
2nd size
2nd size
3rd size
3rd size
4th size
4th size
5th size
5th size
6th size
6th size

CHART 2

16

10

1

all sizes:
work 10-st repeat
15 times
1st size
1st size
2nd size
2nd size
3rd size
3rd size
4th size
4th size
5th size
5th size
6th size
6th size

KEY

☐ = MC
⊡ = A
⊙ = B
⊞ = C
⬤ = D
☒ = E

CHART 3

10

1

all sizes:
work 12-st repeat
13 times
1st size
1st size
2nd size
2nd size
3rd size
3rd size
4th size
4th size
5th size
5th size
6th size
6th size

Sizes

1st size = to fit 38in/97cm bust
2nd size = to fit 40in/102cm bust
3rd size = to fit 42in/107cm bust
4th size = to fit 44in/112cm bust
5th size = to fit 46in/117cm bust
6th size = to fit 48in/122cm bust

SLEEVE CHART

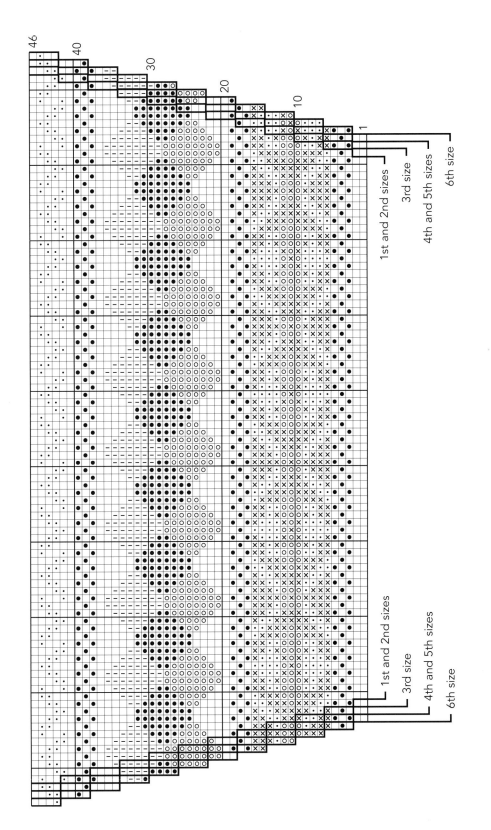

FAIR ISLE SWEATER

YARNS

Rowan Classic *Cashsoft 4-Ply*:

MC Deep 431 10 (10: 11: 11: 12: 12) x 1¾oz/197yd balls
A Kiwi 443 1 (1: 1: 1: 1: 1) x 1¾oz/197yd ball
B Loganberry 430 1 (1: 1: 1: 1: 1) x 1¾oz/197yd ball
C Amethyst 444 1 (1: 1: 1: 1: 1) x 1¾oz/197yd ball
D Navy 440 1 (1: 1: 1: 1: 1) x 1¾oz/197yd ball
E Monet 423 1 (1: 1: 1: 1: 1) x 1¾oz/197yd ball

NEEDLES

Pair of size 2 (3mm) knitting needles
Pair of size 3 (3.25mm) knitting needles
Pair of size 5 (3.75mm) knitting needles
Size 2 (3mm) circular knitting needle

GAUGE

28 sts and 36 rows to 4in/10cm measured over St st using size 3 (3.25mm) needles *or size to obtain correct gauge.*

ABBREVIATIONS

See page 132.

SPECIAL NOTE

When working St st Fair Isle patt from charts, strand yarn not in use loosely across WS of work, weaving it in every 3 or 4 sts. Work odd-numbered chart rows as RS (K) rows, reading them from right to left, and even-numbered rows as WS (P) rows, reading them from left to right.

BACK

Using size 2 (3mm) needles and MC, cast on 162 (168: 176: 182: 190: 196) sts.
Noting that first row is a WS row, work in garter st for 4¾in/12cm, ending with RS facing for next row.
Change to size 5 (3.75mm) needles.
Starting and ending rows as indicated, and joining in and breaking off colors as required, now work in patt from charts (see page 64) as follows:
Work 20 rows from Chart 1, ending with RS facing for next row.
Work 16 rows from Chart 2, ending with RS facing for next row.
Work 10 rows from Chart 3, ending with RS facing for next row.

Break off contrasting colors and cont using MC only.
Change to size 2 (3mm) needles.
Work in garter st for 6 rows, ending with RS facing for next row.
Change to size 3 (3.25mm) needles.
Starting with a K row, work in St st until Back measures 15¾in/40cm from cast-on edge, ending with RS facing for next row.

Shape raglan armholes

Bind off 7 sts at beg of next 2 rows. 148 (154: 162: 168: 176: 182) sts.**
Next row (RS) K2, sl 1, K1, psso, K to last 4 sts, K2tog, K2.
Next row [P2, P2tog] 0 (0: 1: 1: 1: 1) times, P to last 0 (0: 4: 4: 4: 4) sts, [P2tog tbl, P2] 0 (0: 1: 1: 1: 1) times.
Working all raglan armhole decreases as set by last 2 rows, dec 1 st at each end of 3rd (3rd: next: next: next: next) row and foll 0 (0: 2: 4: 10: 14) rows, then on 2 (0: 0: 0: 0: 0) foll 4th rows, then on every foll alt row until 64 (64: 64: 66: 66: 66) sts rem.
Work 1 row, ending with RS facing for next row.

Shape back neck

Next row (RS) K2, sl 1, K1, psso, K4, K2tog and turn, leaving rem sts on a holder.
Work each side of neck separately.
Keeping raglan armhole shaping correct, dec 1 st at each end of 2nd row and foll alt row. 4 sts.
Work 1 row, ending with RS facing for next row.
Next row (RS) K1, sl 1, K2tog, psso.
Next row P2.
Next row K2tog and fasten off.
With RS facing, rejoin yarn to rem sts, bind off center 44 (44: 44: 46: 46: 46) sts, K2tog, K to last 4 sts, K2tog, K2.
Complete to match first side, reversing shapings.

FRONT

Work as given for Back to **.
Working all raglan armhole shaping as set by Back, dec 1 st at each end of next 1 (1: 5: 7: 12: 12) rows, then on 2 (1: 0: 0: 0: 0) foll 4th rows, then on foll 0 (3: 3: 2: 0: 0) alt rows. 142 (144: 146: 150: 152: 158) sts.
Work 3 (1: 1: 1: 0: 0) rows, ending with RS facing for next row.

Divide for neck

Next row (RS) K2, sl 1, K1, psso, K62 (63: 64: 66: 67: 70),

K2tog, K2 and turn, leaving rem sts on a holder.
Work each side of neck separately.

Working all neck decreases in same way as raglan armhole decreases and keeping raglan armhole decreases correct, dec 1 st at raglan armhole edge of 2nd (2nd: 2nd: 2nd: 2nd: next) row and foll 0 (0: 0: 0: 0: 3) rows, then on foll 23 (24: 25: 26: 27: 27) alt rows **and at the same time** dec 1 st at neck edge of 2nd row and every foll alt row. 20 sts.

Dec 1 st at raglan armhole edge only on 2nd row and every foll alt row until 3 sts rem.

Work 1 row, ending with RS facing for next row.

Next row (RS) K1, sl 1, K1, psso.

Next row P2.

Next row K2tog and fasten off.

With RS facing, slip center 2 sts onto a holder, rejoin yarn to rem sts, K2, sl 1, K1, psso, K to last 4 sts, K2tog, K2.

Complete to match first side, reversing shapings.

SLEEVES (make 2)

Using size 2 (3mm) needles and MC, cast on 72 (72: 74: 76: 76: 78) sts.

Noting that first row is a WS row, work in garter st for 4in/10cm, ending with RS facing for next row.

Change to size 5 (3.75mm) needles.

Starting and ending rows as indicated, and joining in and breaking off colors as required, now work in patt from Sleeve Chart (see page 65) as follows:

Inc 1 st at each end of 3rd and 10 foll 4th rows, taking inc sts into patt. 94 (94: 96: 98: 98: 100) sts.

Work 3 rows, ending after chart row 46 and with RS facing for next row.

Break off contrasting colors and cont using MC only.

Change to size 2 (3mm) needles.

Work in garter st for 6 rows, inc 1 st at each end of next row and foll 0 (4th: 4th: 4th: 4th: 4th) of these rows and ending with RS facing for next row.

96 (98: 100: 102: 102: 104) sts.

Change to size 3 (3.25mm) needles.

Starting with a K row, work in St st, inc 1 st at each end of next (3rd: 5th: 5th: 3rd: 3rd) row and 0 (1: 0: 0: 2: 2) foll 4th rows, then on every foll 6th row until there are 114 (116: 118: 120: 122: 124) sts.

Work even until Sleeve measures 17 (17: 17¼: 17¼: 17¼: 17¼)in/43 (43: 44: 44: 44: 44)cm from cast-on edge, ending with RS facing for next row.

Shape raglan

Bind off 7 sts at beg of next 2 rows. 100 (102: 104: 106: 108: 110) sts.

Working all raglan decreases in same way as given for raglan armhole decreases, dec 1 st at each end of next row and 10 foll 4th rows, then on every foll alt row until 22 sts rem.

Work 1 row, ending with RS facing for next row.

Bind off.

FINISHING

Press lightly on WS following instructions on yarn label.

Sew both front and right back raglan seams.

Neckband

With RS facing, using size 2 (3mm) circular needle and MC, pick up and knit 20 sts from top of left sleeve, 60 (62: 64: 66: 68: 70) sts down left side of neck, K 2 sts left on holder at base of V and place a marker between these sts, pick up and knit 60 (62: 64: 66: 68: 70) sts up right side of neck, 20 sts from top of right sleeve, 6 sts down right side of back neck, 44 (44: 44: 46: 46: 46) sts from back, then 6 sts up left side of back neck. 218 (222: 226: 232: 236: 240) sts.

Row 1 (WS) Knit.

Row 2 K to within 2 sts of marker, K2tog, slip marker onto right needle, sl 1, K1, psso, K to end.

Rep last 2 rows 3 times more, and then first of these 2 rows again, ending with RS facing for next row. 210 (214: 218: 224: 228: 232) sts.

Bind off knitwise, still decreasing at each side of marker as before.

Sew side, sleeve seams and right front raglan seam.

striped scarf

WENDY BAKER

SIZE
The finished scarf measures approximately 7¾in/20cm by 94½in/240cm.

YARNS
1 x 1¾oz/197yd ball of Rowan Classic *Cashsoft 4-Ply* in each of **A** (Deep 431), **B** (Kiwi 443), **C** (Loganberry 430), **D** (Amethyst 444), and **E** (Navy 440)

NEEDLES
Pair of size 3 (3.25mm) knitting needles

GAUGE
28 sts and 36 rows to 4in/10cm measured over St st using size 3 (3.25mm) needles *or size to obtain correct gauge.*

ABBREVIATIONS
See page 132.

SCARF
First Section
Using size 3 (3.25mm) needles and A, cast on 56 sts. Starting with a K row and joining in and breaking off colors as required, work in St st in stripes as follows:

Rows 1–84 Using A.
Rows 85–93 Using B.
Rows 94–102 Using E.
Rows 103 and 104 Using C.
Rows 105–108 Using A.
Rows 109–120 Using C.
Rows 121–126 Using B.
Rows 127–162 Using E.

Rows 163–198 Using B.
Rows 199–234 Using C.
Rows 235–270 Using D.
Rows 271–306 Using A.
Rows 307–342 Using B.
Rows 343–378 Using D.
Rows 379–414 Using C.
Rows 415–432 Using E.
Break off yarn and leave sts on a holder.

Second section
Work as given for First Section until row 431 has been completed, ending with WS facing for next row.

Join sections
Holding RS of First Section against RS of Second Section, bind off both sets of sts at same time, taking one st from one section with corresponding st of other section.

FINISHING
Press lightly on WS following instructions on yarn label.

wrap jacket

MARTIN STOREY

TO FIT BUST

38	40	42	44	46	48	in
97	102	107	112	117	122	cm

FINISHED MEASUREMENTS

Around bust

45	46¾	49¼	51	53	55½	in
114	119	125	130	135	141	cm

Length to back neck

20¾	21¼	21½	22	22½	22¾	in
53	54	55	56	57	58	cm

Sleeve seam

7½	7½	7¾	7¾	7¾	7¾	in
19	19	20	20	20	20	cm

YARN

12 (13: 13: 14: 15: 15) x 1¾oz/109yd balls of Rowan Classic *Silk Wool DK* in Velvet 307

NEEDLES

Pair of size 6 (4mm) knitting needles
Size 3 (3.25mm) circular knitting needle

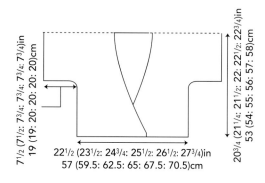

7½ (7½: 7¾: 7¾: 7¾: 7¾)in
19 (19: 20: 20: 20: 20)cm

22½ (23½: 24¾: 25½: 26½: 27¾)in
57 (59.5: 62.5: 65: 67.5: 70.5)cm

20¾ (21¼: 21½: 22: 22½: 22¾)in
53 (54: 55: 56: 57: 58)cm

GAUGE

22 sts and 30 rows to 4in/10cm measured over St st using size 6 (4mm) needles *or size to obtain correct gauge.*

ABBREVIATIONS

See page 132.

LEFT FRONT

Using size 6 (4mm) needles, cast on 73 (76: 79: 82: 85: 88) sts.

Starting with a K row, work in St st for 4 rows, ending with RS facing for next row.

Shape front slope

Dec 1 st at end of next row and 17 (17: 17: 18: 17: 16) foll 4th rows, then on 0 (0: 1: 0: 1: 2) foll 6th rows. 55 (58: 60: 63: 66: 69) sts.

Work 3 (3: 1: 3: 3: 1) rows, ending with RS facing for next row.

Shape for sleeve

Inc 1 st at beg of next row and foll 2 alt rows, then at same edge on foll 2 rows **and at the same time** dec 1 st at front slope edge on next (next: 5th: next: 3rd: 5th) row and foll 4th (4th: 0: 6th: 0: 0) row. 58 (61: 64: 66: 70: 73) sts.

Work 1 row, ending with RS facing for next row.

Cast on 16 sts at beg of next row, then 16 (16: 18: 18: 18: 18) sts at beg of foll alt row **and at the same time** dec 1 st at front slope edge on next (3rd: 3rd: 0: next: 3rd) of these rows. 89 (92: 97: 100: 103: 106) sts.

Dec 1 st at front slope edge only on 4th (6th: 6th: 2nd: 4th: 6th) row and every foll 6th row until 78 (81: 86: 88: 91: 94) sts rem.

Work 9 rows, ending with RS facing for next row.
Break off yarn and leave sts on a holder.

RIGHT FRONT

Using size 6 (4mm) needles, cast on 73 (76: 79: 82: 85: 88) sts.

Starting with a K row, work in St st for 4 rows, ending with RS facing for next row.

Shape front slope

Dec 1 st at beg of next row and 17 (17: 17: 18: 17: 16) foll 4th rows, then on 0 (0: 1: 0: 1: 2) foll 6th rows. 55 (58: 60: 63: 66: 69) sts.

Complete as given for Left Front, reversing shapings.

BACK

With RS facing and using size 6 (4mm) needles,
K across 78 (81: 86: 88: 91: 94) sts of Left Front, cast on 43 (43: 43: 45: 45: 45) sts onto right needle, K across 78 (81: 86: 88: 91: 94) sts of Right Front. 199 (205: 215: 221: 227: 233) sts.

Starting with a P row, work in St st for 73 (75: 75: 77: 79: 81) rows, ending with RS facing for next row.

Shape for sleeves

Bind off 16 (16: 18: 18: 18: 18) sts at beg of next 2 rows, then 16 sts at beg of foll 2 rows. 135 (141: 147: 153: 159: 165) sts.

Dec 1 st at each end of next 3 rows, then on foll 2 alt rows. 125 (131: 137: 143: 149: 155) sts.

Work 75 (75: 79: 79: 81: 81) rows, ending with RS facing for next row.

Bind off.

FINISHING

Press lightly on WS following instructions on yarn label.

Front band

With RS facing and using size 3 (3.25mm) circular needle, starting and ending at front cast-on edges, pick up and knit 140 (142: 144: 147: 149: 151) sts up right front opening edge to back neck cast-on sts, 48 (48: 48: 50: 50: 50) sts from back neck, then 140 (142: 144: 147: 149: 151) sts down left front opening edge. 328 (332: 336: 344: 348: 352) sts.

Starting with a P row, work in St st for 3in/8cm, ending with RS facing for next row.

Bind off.

Sleeve bands (both alike)

With RS facing and using size 3 (3.25mm) circular needle, pick up and knit 118 (122: 122: 126: 130: 134) sts along row-end edge of sleeve section.

Starting with a P row, work in St st for 2¼in/6cm, ending with RS facing for next row.

Bind off.

Sew side and sleeve seams, reversing sleeve seam for sleeve band roll.

lace tunic

MARTIN STOREY

TO FIT BUST

38	40	42	44	46	48	in
97	102	107	112	117	122	cm

FINISHED MEASUREMENTS

Around bust

45	46½	48½	50½	52¼	54¼	in
114	118	123	128	133	138	cm

Length to back neck

28¼	28¾	29	29½	30	30¼	in
72	73	74	75	76	77	cm

Sleeve seam

13	13	13¼	13¼	13¼	13¼	in
33	33	34	34	34	34	cm

YARN

6 (7: 7: 7: 8: 8) x ⅞oz/229yd balls of Rowan *Kidsilk Haze* in Trance 582

NEEDLES

Pair of size 2 (2.75mm) knitting needles
Pair of size 3 (3.25mm) knitting needles

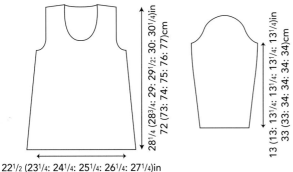

22½ (23¼: 24¼: 25¼: 26¼: 27¼)in
57 (59: 61.5: 64: 66.5: 69)cm

28¼ (28¾: 29: 29½: 30: 30¼)in
72 (73: 74: 75: 76: 77)cm

13 (13: 13¼: 13¼: 13¼: 13¼)in
33 (33: 34: 34: 34: 34)cm

GAUGE

25 sts and 34 rows to 4in/10cm measured over patt using size 3 (3.25mm) needles *or size to obtain correct gauge.*

ABBREVIATIONS

See page 132.

BACK

Using size 3 (3.25mm) needles, cast on 168 (174: 180: 186: 192: 198) sts.
Row 1 (RS) Knit.
Row 2 and every foll alt row Purl.
Row 3 K3 (6: 9: 2: 5: 8), yo, K2tog, *K8, yo, K2tog; rep from * to last 3 (6: 9: 2: 5: 8) sts, K3 (6: 9: 2: 5: 8).
Row 5 Knit.
Row 7 Knit.
Row 9 K8 (1: 4: 7: 10: 3), yo, K2tog, *K8, yo, K2tog; rep from * to last 8 (1: 4: 7: 10: 3) sts, K8 (1: 4: 7: 10: 3).
Row 11 K2tog, K to last 2 sts, K2tog.
Row 12 Purl.
These last 12 rows form patt and start side seam shaping.
Keeping patt correct, dec 1 st at each end of 11th row and every foll 12th row until 142 (148: 154: 160: 166: 172) sts rem.
Work even until Back measures 19¼ (19¼: 19½: 19½: 20: 20)in/49 (49: 50: 50: 51: 51)cm from cast-on edge, ending with RS facing for next row.
Shape armholes
Keeping patt correct, bind off 10 (11: 11: 12: 12: 13) sts at beg of next 2 rows. 122 (126: 132: 136: 142: 146) sts.**
Dec 1 st at each end of next 5 (5: 7: 7: 9: 9) rows, then

on foll 3 (4: 4: 5: 5: 6) alt rows, then on 2 foll 4th rows. 102 (104: 106: 108: 110: 112) sts.

Work even until armhole measures 8½ (9: 9: 9½: 9½: 9¾)in/22 (23: 23: 24: 24: 25)cm, ending with RS facing for next row.

Shape back neck and shoulders

Bind off 9 (9: 10: 10: 10: 10) sts at beg of next 2 rows. 84 (86: 86: 88: 90: 92) sts.

Next row (RS) Bind off 9 (9: 10: 10: 10: 10) sts, patt until there are 13 (14: 13: 13: 14: 15) sts on right needle and turn, leaving rem sts on a holder.

Work each side of neck separately.

Bind off 4 sts at beg of next row.

Bind off rem 9 (10: 9: 9: 10: 11) sts.

With RS facing, rejoin yarn to rem sts, bind off center 40 (40: 40: 42: 42: 42) sts, patt to end.

Complete to match first side, reversing shapings.

FRONT

Work as given for Back to **.

Dec 1 st at each end of next 5 (5: 7: 7: 9: 9) rows, then on foll 3 (4: 3: 3: 2: 2) alt rows. 106 (108: 112: 116: 120: 124) sts.

Work 3 (1: 1: 1: 1: 1) rows, ending with RS facing for next row.

Shape neck

Next row (RS) [K2tog] 1 (0: 1: 1: 1: 1) times, patt 40 (43: 43: 44: 46: 48) sts and turn, leaving rem sts on a holder.

Work each side of neck separately.

Keeping patt correct, dec 1 st at neck edge of next 6 rows, then on foll 4 alt rows, then on 3 foll 4th rows **and at the same time** dec 1 st at armhole edge of 4th (2nd: 4th: 2nd: 2nd: 2nd) and foll 0 (0: 0: 0: 1: 2) alt rows, then on 0 (1: 1: 2: 2: 2) foll 4th rows. 27 (28: 29: 29: 30: 31) sts.

Work even until Left Front matches Back to start of shoulder shaping, ending with RS facing for next row.

Shape shoulder

Bind off 9 (9: 10: 10: 10: 10) sts at beg of next row and foll alt row.

Work 1 row.

Bind off rem 9 (10: 9: 9: 10: 11) sts.

With RS facing, rejoin yarn to rem sts, bind off center 22 (22: 22: 24: 24: 24) sts, patt to end.

Complete to match first side, reversing shapings.

SLEEVES (make 2)

Using size 3 (3.25mm) needles, cast on 84 (84: 86: 88: 88: 90) sts.

Row 1 (RS) Knit.

Row 2 and every foll alt row Purl.

Row 3 K1 (1: 2: 3: 3: 4), yo, K2tog, *K8, yo, K2tog; rep from * to last 1 (1: 2: 3: 3: 4) sts, K1 (1: 2: 3: 3: 4).

Row 5 Knit.

Row 7 Knit.

Row 9 K6 (6: 7: 8: 8: 9), yo, K2tog, *K8, yo, K2tog; rep from * to last 6 (6: 7: 8: 8: 9) sts, K6 (6: 7: 8: 8: 9).

Row 11 Knit.

Row 12 Purl.

These 12 rows form patt.

Work in patt for 4 rows more, ending with RS facing for next row.

Inc 1 st at each end of next row and every foll 16th (12th: 12th: 12th: 10th: 10th) row until there are 96 (90: 90: 92: 92: 94) sts, taking inc sts into patt.

40, 42, 44, 46, and 48in sizes only

Inc 1 st at each end of next row and every foll (14th: 14th: 14th: 12th: 12th) row until there are (98: 100: 102: 104: 106) sts.

All sizes

Work even until Sleeve measures 13 (13: 13¼: 13¼: 13¼: 13¼)in/33 (33: 34: 34: 34: 34)cm from cast-on edge, ending with RS facing for next row.

Shape top of sleeve

Keeping patt correct, bind off 10 (11: 11: 12: 12: 13) sts at beg of next 2 rows. 76 (76: 78: 78: 80: 80) sts.

Dec 1 st at each end of next 3 rows, then on foll 6 alt rows, then on every foll 4th row until 52 (52: 54: 54: 56: 56) sts rem.

Work 1 row.

Dec 1 st at each end of next row and every foll alt row until 32 sts rem, then on foll 3 rows, ending with RS facing for next row.

Bind off rem 26 sts.

FINISHING

Press lightly on WS following instructions on yarn label. Sew shoulder seams. Sew sleeves into armholes. Sew side and sleeve seams.

Neck trim

Using size 2 (2.75mm) needles, cast on 3 sts.

LACE TUNIC

Row 1 (WS) P3.

Row 2 K1, yo, K1 tbl, P1. 4 sts.

Row 3 P2, [K1, P1] twice into yo of previous row, P1. 7 sts.

Row 4 Bind off 4 sts (one st on right needle after bind-off), K1 tbl, P1. 3 sts.

These 4 rows form patt.

Work in patt until Neck Trim fits around entire neck edge, ending after a patt row 4 and with WS facing for next row.

Bind off.

Sew together ends of Trim, then sew straight edge in place around neck edge.

Cuff trims (both alike)

Work as given for Neck Trim, making and sewing on a strip to fit around cast-on edge of Sleeve.

Hem trim

Work as given for Neck Trim, making and sewing on a strip to fit around entire cast-on edge of Back and Front.

lacy cardigan

KIM HARGREAVES

TO FIT BUST

38	40	42	44	46	48	in
97	102	107	112	117	122	cm

FINISHED MEASUREMENTS

Around bust

41¼	43	44¾	46¾	48¾	50¼	in
105	109	114	119	124	128	cm

Length to shoulder

22¾	23¼	23½	24	24½	24¾	in
58	59	60	61	62	63	cm

Sleeve seam

17	17	17¼	17¼	17¼	17¼	in
43	43	44	44	44	44	cm

YARN

11 (12: 12: 13: 13: 14) x 1¾oz/186yd balls of Rowan *4-Ply Cotton* in Cream 153

NEEDLES

Pair of size 3 (3mm) knitting needles
Size 1 (2.25mm) circular knitting needle

EXTRAS

7 buttons

GAUGE

34 sts and 38 rows to 4in/10cm measured over patt using size 3 (3mm) needles *or size to obtain correct gauge.*

ABBREVIATIONS

See page 132.

BACK

Using size 1 (2.25mm) circular needle, cast on 533 (557: 581: 605: 629: 653) sts.

Row 1 (RS) K1, *K2, lift first of these 2 sts over 2nd st and off right needle; rep from * to end. 267 (279: 291: 303: 315: 327) sts.

Row 2 *P1, P2tog; rep from * to end. 178 (186: 194: 202: 210: 218) sts.

These 2 rows form frill edging.

Change to size 3 (3mm) needles.

Now work in patt as follows:

Row 1 (RS) K0 (1: 2: 0: 1: 2), [P1, yo, K2tog tbl] 0 (1: 0: 0: 1: 0) times, P1, *K2, P1, yo, K2tog tbl, P1; rep from * to last 3 (1: 5: 3: 1: 5) sts, K2 (1: 2: 2: 1: 2), P1 (0: 1: 1: 0: 1), K0 (0: 2: 0: 0: 2).

Row 2 P0 (1: 2: 0: 1: 2), K1, *P2, K1; rep from * to last 0 (1: 2: 0: 1: 2) sts, P0 (1: 2: 0: 1: 2).

Row 3 K0 (1: 2: 0: 1: 2), [P1, K2tog, yo] 0 (1: 0: 0: 1: 0) times, P1, *K2, P1, K2tog, yo, P1; rep from * to last 3 (1: 5: 3: 1: 5) sts, K2 (1: 2: 2: 1: 2), P1 (0: 1: 1: 0: 1), K0 (0: 2: 0: 0: 2).

Row 4 Rep row 2.

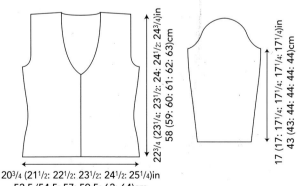

20¾ (21½: 22½: 23½: 24½: 25¼)in
52.5 (54.5: 57: 59.5: 62: 64)cm

22¾ (23¾: 23½: 24: 24½: 24¾)in
58 (59: 60: 61: 62: 63)cm

17 (17: 17¼: 17¼: 17¼: 17¼)in
43 (43: 44: 44: 44: 44)cm

These 4 rows form patt.

Work in patt for 18 rows more, ending with RS facing for next row.

Keeping patt correct, dec 1 st at each end of next row and every foll 4th row until 162 (170: 178: 186: 194: 202) sts rem.

Work even until Back measures 7 (7: 7½: 7½: 7¾: 7¾)in/18 (18: 19: 19: 20: 20)cm from cast-on edge, ending with RS facing for next row.

Inc 1 st at each end of next row and every foll 8th row until there are 178 (186: 194: 202: 210: 218) sts, taking inc sts into patt.

Work 19 rows, ending with RS facing for next row.

Shape armholes

Keeping patt correct, bind off 6 (6: 7: 7: 8: 8) sts at beg of next 2 rows, then 3 sts at beg of foll 2 rows. 160 (168: 174: 182: 188: 196) sts.

Dec 1 st at each end of next 7 (9: 9: 11: 11: 13) rows, then on foll 9 (9: 10: 10: 11: 11) alt rows, then on 6 foll 4th rows. 116 (120: 124: 128: 132: 136) sts.

Work even until armhole measures 7¾ (8¼: 8¼: 8½: 8½: 9)in/20 (21: 21: 22: 22: 23)cm, ending with RS facing for next row.

Shape back neck and shoulders

Bind off 10 (10: 11: 11: 12: 13) sts at beg of next 2 rows. 96 (100: 102: 106: 108: 110) sts.

Next row (RS) Bind off 10 (10: 11: 11: 12: 13) sts, patt until there are 13 (15: 15: 16: 16: 16) sts on right needle and turn, leaving rem sts on a holder.

Work each side of neck separately.

Bind off 4 sts at beg of next row.

Bind off rem 9 (11: 11: 12: 12: 12) sts.

With RS facing, rejoin yarn to rem sts, bind off center 50 (50: 50: 52: 52: 52) sts, patt to end.

Complete to match first side, reversing shapings.

LEFT FRONT

Using size 1 (2.25mm) circular needle, cast on 263 (275: 287: 299: 311: 323) sts.

Work frill edging rows 1 and 2 as given for Back. 88 (92: 96: 100: 104: 108) sts.

Change to size 3 (3mm) needles.

Now work in patt as follows:

Row 1 (RS) K0 (1: 2: 0: 1: 2), [P1, yo, K2tog tbl] 0 (1: 0: 0: 1: 0) times, P1, *K2, P1, yo, K2tog tbl, P1; rep from * to

last 3 sts, K2, P1.

Row 2 K1, *P2, K1; rep from * to last 0 (1: 2: 0: 1: 2) sts, P0 (1: 2: 0: 1: 2).

Row 3 K0 (1: 2: 0: 1: 2), [P1, K2tog, yo] 0 (1: 0: 0: 1: 0) times, P1, *K2, P1, K2tog, yo, P1; rep from * to last 3 sts, K2, P1.

Row 4 Rep row 2.

These 4 rows form patt.

Work in patt for 18 rows more, ending with RS facing for next row.

Keeping patt correct, dec 1 st at beg of next row and every foll 4th row until 80 (84: 88: 92: 96: 100) sts rem.

Work even until Left Front measures 7 (7: 7½: 7½: 7¾: 7¾)in/18 (18: 19: 19: 20: 20)cm from cast-on edge, ending with RS facing for next row.

Inc 1 st at beg of next row and every foll 8th row until there are 88 (92: 96: 100: 104: 108) sts, taking inc sts into patt.

Work 5 rows, ending with RS facing for next row.

Shape front slope

Keeping patt correct, dec 1 st at end of next row and foll 5 alt rows. 82 (86: 90: 94: 98: 102) sts.

Work 1 row, ending with RS facing for next row.

Shape armhole

Keeping patt correct, bind off 6 (6: 7: 7: 8: 8) sts at beg of next row, then 3 sts at beg of foll alt row **and at the same time** dec 1 st at front slope edge of next row and foll alt row. 71 (75: 78: 82: 85: 89) sts.

Work 1 row.

Dec 1 st at armhole edge of next 7 (9: 9: 11: 11: 13) rows, then on foll 9 (9: 10: 10: 11: 11) alt rows, then on 6 foll 4th rows **and at the same time** dec 1 st at front slope edge of next row and foll 8 (6: 6: 6: 6: 4) alt rows, then on every foll 4th row. 32 (35: 36: 38: 39: 42) sts.

Dec 1 st at front slope edge only on 4th (2nd: 4th: 2nd: 4th: 2nd) row and every foll 4th row until 29 (31: 33: 34: 36: 38) sts rem.

Work even until Left Front matches Back to start of shoulder shaping, ending with RS facing for next row.

Shape shoulder

Bind off 10 (10: 11: 11: 12: 13) sts at beg of next row and foll alt row.

Work 1 row.

Bind off rem 9 (11: 11: 12: 12: 12) sts.

KNITTING GOES LARGE

RIGHT FRONT

Using size 1 (2.25mm) circular needle, cast on 263 (275: 287: 299: 311: 323) sts.

Work frill edging rows 1 and 2 as given for Back. 88 (92: 96: 100: 104: 108) sts.

Change to size 3 (3mm) needles.

Now work in patt as follows:

Row 1 (RS) P1, *K2, P1, yo, K2tog tbl, P1; rep from * to last 3 (1: 5: 3: 1: 5) sts, K2 (1: 2: 2: 1: 2), P1 (0: 1: 1: 0: 1), K0 (0: 2: 0: 0: 2).

Row 2 P0 (1: 2: 0: 1: 2), K1, *P2, K1; rep from * to end.

Row 3 P1, *K2, P1, K2tog, yo, P1; rep from * to last 3 (1: 5: 3: 1: 5) sts, K2 (1: 2: 2: 1: 2), P1 (0: 1: 1: 0: 1), K0 (0: 2: 0: 0: 2).

Row 4 Rep row 2.

These 4 rows form patt.

Work in patt for 18 rows more, ending with RS facing for next row.

Keeping patt correct, dec 1 st at end of next row and every foll 4th row until 80 (84: 88: 92: 96: 100) sts rem.

Complete to match Left Front, reversing shapings.

SLEEVES (make 2)

Using size 1 (2.25mm) circular needle, cast on 257 (257: 263: 269: 269: 275) sts.

Work frill edging rows 1 and 2 as given for Back. 86 (86: 88: 90: 90: 92) sts.

Change to size 3 (3mm) needles.

Now work in patt as follows:

Row 1 (RS) K2 (2: 0: 1: 1: 2), [P1, yo, K2tog tbl] 0 (0: 1: 1: 1: 1) times, P1, *K2, P1, yo, K2tog tbl, P1; rep from * to last 5 (5: 0: 1: 1: 2) sts, K2 (2: 0: 1: 1: 2), [P1, K2] 1 (1: 0: 0: 0: 0) times.

Row 2 P2 (2: 0: 1: 1: 2), K1, *P2, K1; rep from * to last 2 (2: 0: 1: 1: 2) sts, P2 (2: 0: 1: 1: 2).

Row 3 K2 (2: 0: 1: 1: 2), [P1, K2tog, yo] 0 (0: 1: 1: 1: 1) times, P1, *K2, P1, K2tog, yo, P1; rep from * to last 5 (5: 0: 1: 1: 2) sts, K2 (2: 0: 1: 1: 2), [P1, K2] 1 (1: 0: 0: 0: 0) times.

Row 4 Rep row 2.

These 4 rows form patt.

Work in patt, shaping sides by inc 1 st at each end of 3rd (3rd: 3rd: 3rd: next: next) row and every foll 8th (8th: 8th: 8th: 6th: 6th) row until there are 112 (122: 120: 122: 94: 96) sts, taking inc sts into patt.

38, 42, 44, 46, and 48in sizes only

Inc 1 st at each end of every foll 10th (10th: 10th: 8th: 8th) row until there are 120 (124: 126: 128: 130) sts.

All sizes

Work even until Sleeve measures 17 (17: 17¼: 17¼: 17¼: 17¼)in/43 (43: 44: 44: 44: 44)cm from cast-on edge, ending with RS facing for next row.

Shape top of sleeve

Keeping patt correct, bind off 6 (6: 7: 7: 8: 8) sts at beg of next 2 rows. 108 (110: 110: 112: 112: 114) sts.

Dec 1 st at each end of next 5 rows, then on foll 5 alt rows, then on every foll 4th row until 74 (76: 76: 78: 78: 80) sts rem.

Work 1 row.

Dec 1 st at each end of next row and every foll alt row until 62 sts rem, then on foll 7 rows, ending with RS facing for next row. 48 sts.

Bind off 8 sts at beg of next 2 rows.

Bind off rem 32 sts.

FINISHING

Press lightly on WS following instructions on yarn label.

Sew shoulder seams.

Front band

With RS facing and using size 1 (2.25mm) circular needles, starting and ending at cast-on edges, pick up and knit 102 (102: 105: 105: 108: 108) sts up right front opening edge to start of front slope shaping, place marker on right needle, 78 (81: 81: 85: 85: 88) sts up right front slope to shoulder, 58 (58: 58: 60: 60: 60) sts from back, 78 (81: 81: 85: 85: 88) sts down left front slope to start of front slope shaping, then 102 (102: 105: 105: 108: 108) sts down left front opening edge. 418 (424: 430: 440: 446: 452) sts.

Row 1 (WS) K to marker, slip marker onto right needle, K2 (2: 0: 0: 2: 2), *K2tog, yo (to make a buttonhole), K14 (14: 15: 15: 15: 15); rep from * 5 times more, K2tog, yo (to make 7th buttonhole), K2 (2: 1: 1: 2: 2).

Row 2 Knit.

Bind off knitwise (on WS).

Sew sleeves into armholes. Sew side and sleeve seams.

Sew on buttons.

swing jackets

CATHERINE TOUGH

TO FIT BUST

38	40	42	44	46	48	in
97	102	107	112	117	122	cm

FINISHED MEASUREMENTS

Around bust

43¼	45¼	47½	49½	52	54	in
110	115	121	126	132	137	cm

Length to shoulder

Longer version

30¾	31	31½	32	32¼	32½	in
78	79	80	81	82	83	cm

Shorter version

25	25½	26	26¼	26¾	27½	in
64	65	66	67	68	70	cm

Sleeve seam

17¼	17¼	17¾	17¾	17¾	17¾	in
44	44	45	45	45	45	cm

YARN

Longer version

19 (20: 21: 22: 23: 24) x 1¾oz/109yd balls of Rowan Classic *Baby Alpaca DK* in Cheviot 207

Shorter version

18 (18: 19: 20: 21: 22) x 1¾oz/109yd balls of Rowan Classic *Baby Alpaca DK* in Chambray 201

NEEDLES

Pair of size 5 (3.75mm) knitting needles

EXTRAS

1 toggle button

GAUGE

22 sts and 40 rows to 4in/10cm measured over garter st using size 5 (3.75mm) needles *or size to obtain correct gauge.*

ABBREVIATIONS

See page 132.

longer version

BACK

Using size 5 (3.75mm) needles, cast on 143 (149: 155: 161: 167: 173) sts.

Noting that first row is a WS row, work in garter st for 15 rows, ending with RS facing for next row.

Row 16 (RS) K10, sl 1, K1, psso, K to last 12 sts, K2tog, K10.

Work 15 rows.

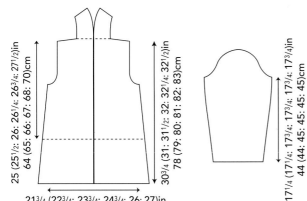

25 (25½: 26: 26¼: 26¾: 27½)in
64 (65: 66: 67: 68: 70)cm

30¾ (31: 31½: 32: 32¼: 32½)in
78 (79: 80: 81: 82: 83)cm

17¼ (17¼: 17¾: 17¾: 17¾: 17¾)in
44 (44: 45: 45: 45: 45)cm

21¾ (22¾: 23¾: 24¾: 26: 27)in
55 (57.5: 60.5: 63: 66: 68.5)cm

Rep last 16 rows 9 times more, then row 16 again.
121 (127: 133: 139: 145: 151) sts.

Work even until Back measures 21½ (21½: 22: 22: 22½: 22½)in/55 (55: 56: 56: 57: 57)cm from cast-on edge, ending with RS facing for next row.

Shape armholes

Bind off 8 (8: 9: 9: 10: 10) sts at beg of next 2 rows.
105 (111: 115: 121: 125: 131) sts.

Next row (RS) K2, sl 1, K1, psso, K to last 4 sts, K2tog, K2.

Next row K2, K2tog, K to last 4 sts, sl 1, K1, psso, K2.

Working all armhole decreases as set by last 2 rows, dec 1 st at each end of next 1 (3: 3: 5: 5: 7) rows, then on foll 8 (8: 9: 9: 10: 10) alt rows. 83 (85: 87: 89: 91: 93) sts.

Work even until armhole measures 9 (9½: 9½: 9¾: 9¾: 10¼)in/23 (24: 24: 25: 25: 26)cm, ending with RS facing for next row.

Shape shoulders

Bind off 8 (8: 9: 9: 9: 9) sts at beg of next 4 rows, then 8 (9: 8: 8: 9: 10) sts at beg of foll 2 rows.

Bind off rem 35 (35: 35: 37: 37: 37) sts.

LEFT FRONT

Using size 5 (3.75mm) needles, cast on 67 (70: 73: 76: 79: 82) sts.

Noting that first row is a WS row, work in garter st for 15 rows, ending with RS facing for next row.

Row 16 (RS) K8, sl 1, K1, psso, K to last 6 sts, M1, K6.

Work 15 rows.

Rep last 16 rows 9 times more, then row 16 again. 67 (70: 73: 76: 79: 82) sts.

**Work even until Left Front matches Back to start of armhole shaping, ending with RS facing for next row.

Shape armhole

Bind off 8 (8: 9: 9: 10: 10) sts at beg of next row. 59 (62: 64: 67: 69: 72) sts.

Work 1 row.

Working all armhole decreases as set by Back, dec 1 st at armhole edge of next 3 (5: 5: 7: 7: 9) rows, then on foll 8 (8: 9: 9: 10: 10) alt rows. 48 (49: 50: 51: 52: 53) sts.

Work even until Left Front matches Back to start of shoulder shaping, ending with RS facing for next row.

Shape shoulder

Bind off 8 (8: 9: 9: 9: 9) sts at beg of next row and foll alt row, then 8 (9: 8: 8: 9: 10) sts at beg of foll alt row, ending with WS facing for next row. 24 (24: 24: 25: 25: 25) sts.

Shape collar extension

Next row K to last 10 sts, wrap next st (by slipping next st from left needle onto right needle, taking yarn to opposite side of work between needles and then slipping same st back onto left needle—when working across wrapped sts, K tog the wrapped st and the wrapping loop) and turn.

Next row Knit to end.

Work 4 rows.

Rep last 6 rows 10 (10: 10: 11: 11: 11) times more.

Bind off.

RIGHT FRONT

Using size 5 (3.75mm) needles, cast on 67 (70: 73: 76: 79: 82) sts.

Noting that first row is a WS row, work in garter st for 15 rows, ending with RS facing for next row.

Row 16 (RS) K6, M1, K to last 10 sts, K2tog, K8.

Work 15 rows.

Rep last 16 rows 9 times more, then row 16 again. 67 (70: 73: 76: 79: 82) sts.

**Work even until Right Front matches Back to start of armhole shaping, ending with RS facing for next row.

Next row (buttonhole row) (RS) K5, K2tog, [yo] twice (to make a buttonhole, on next row work into front and back of this double yo), sl 1, K1, psso, K to end.

Shape armhole

Bind off 8 (8: 9: 9: 10: 10) sts at beg of next row. 59 (62: 64: 67: 69: 72) sts.

Working all armhole decreases as set by Back, dec 1 st at armhole edge of next 3 (5: 5: 7: 7: 9) rows, then on foll 8 (8: 9: 9: 10: 10) alt rows. 48 (49: 50: 51: 52: 53) sts.

Work even until Right Front matches Back to start of shoulder shaping, ending with WS facing for next row.

Shape shoulder

Bind off 8 (8: 9: 9: 9: 9) sts at beg of next row and foll alt row, then 8 (9: 8: 8: 9: 10) sts at beg of foll alt row, ending with RS facing for next row. 24 (24: 24: 25: 25: 25) sts.

Shape collar extension

Next row K to last 10 sts, wrap next st (by slipping next st from left needle onto right needle, taking yarn to opposite side of work between needles and then slipping same st back onto left needle—when working across wrapped sts, K tog the wrapped st and the wrapping loop) and turn.

Next row Knit to end.

Work 4 rows.

Rep last 6 rows 10 (10: 10: 11: 11: 11) times more.

Bind off.

SLEEVES (make 2)

Using size 5 (3.75mm) needles, cast on 60 (60: 62: 64: 64: 66) sts.

Noting that first row is a WS row, work in garter st for 21 rows, ending with RS facing for next row.

Row 22 (RS) K4, M1, K to last 4 sts, M1, K4.

Working all increases as set by last row, inc 1 st at each end of every foll 12th (12th: 12th: 12th: 10th: 10th) row to 66 (80: 78: 80: 70: 72) sts, then on every foll 14th (14th: 14th: 14th: 12th: 12th) row until there are 82 (84: 86: 88: 90: 92) sts.

Work even until Sleeve measures 17¼ (17¼: 17¾: 17¾: 17¾: 17¾)in/44 (44: 45: 45: 45: 45)cm from cast-on edge, ending with RS facing for next row.

Shape top of sleeve

Bind off 8 (8: 9: 9: 10: 10) sts at beg of next 2 rows. 66 (68: 68: 70: 70: 72) sts.

Working all decreases in same way as armhole decreases, dec 1 st at each end of 3rd row and every foll 4th row until 36 (38: 38: 40: 40: 42) sts rem, then on every foll alt row until 24 sts rem.

Work 1 row, ending with RS facing for next row.

Bind off 3 sts at beg of next 4 rows.

Bind off rem 12 sts.

FINISHING

Press lightly on WS following instructions on yarn label. Sew shoulder seams. Sew together bound-off edges of collar extensions, then sew one edge of collar extensions to back neck edge.

Sew sleeves into armholes. Sew side and sleeve seams. Sew on toggle button.

shorter version

BACK

Using size 5 (3.75mm) needles, cast on 139 (145: 151: 157: 163: 169) sts.

Noting that first row is a WS row, work in garter st for

---

15 rows, ending with RS facing for next row.

Row 16 (RS) K10, sl 1, K1, psso, K to last 12 sts, K2tog, K10.

Work 15 rows.

Rep last 16 rows 7 times more, then row 16 again. 121 (127: 133: 139: 145: 151) sts.

Work even until Back measures 16 (16: 16½: 16½: 17: 17)in/41 (41: 42: 42: 43: 43)cm from cast-on edge, ending with RS facing for next row.

Complete as given for Back of Longer Version from start of armhole shaping.

LEFT FRONT

Using size 5 (3.75mm) needles, cast on 67 (70: 73: 76: 79: 82) sts.

Noting that first row is a WS row, work in garter st for 15 rows, ending with RS facing for next row.

Row 16 (RS) K8, sl 1, K1, psso, K to last 6 sts, M1, K6.

Work 15 rows.

Rep last 16 rows 7 times more, then row 16 again. 67 (70: 73: 76: 79: 82) sts.

Complete as given for Left Front of Longer Version from **.

RIGHT FRONT

Using size 5 (3.75mm) needles, cast on 67 (70: 73: 76: 79: 82) sts.

Noting that first row is a WS row, work in garter st for 15 rows, ending with RS facing for next row.

Row 16 (RS) K6, M1, K to last 10 sts, K2tog, K8.

Work 15 rows.

Rep last 16 rows 7 times more, then row 16 again. 67 (70: 73: 76: 79: 82) sts.

Complete as given for Right Front of Longer Version from **.

SLEEVES (make 2)

Work as given for Sleeves of Longer Version.

FINISHING

Work as given for Longer Version.

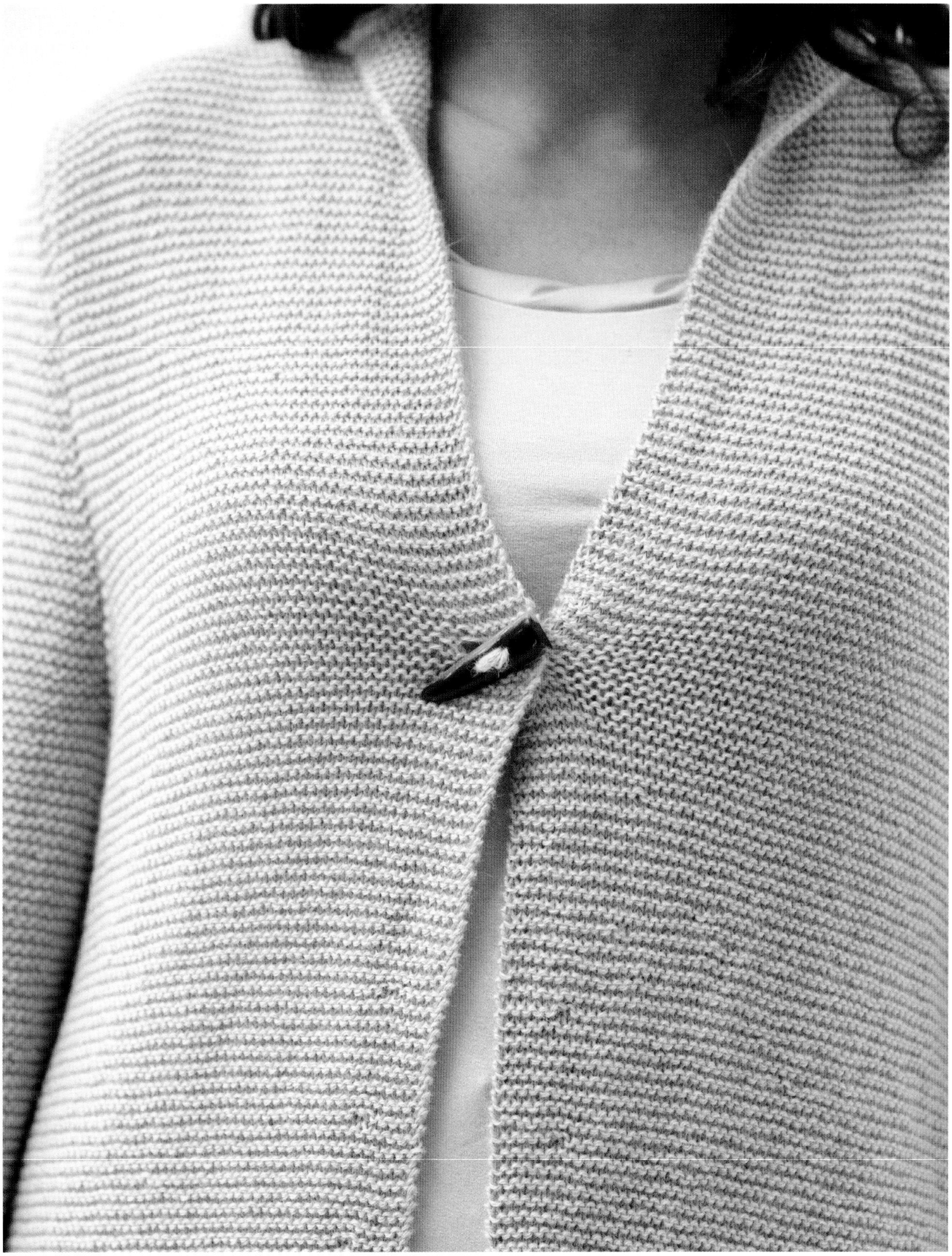

textured top

KIM HARGREAVES

TO FIT BUST						
38	40	42	44	46	48	in
97	102	107	112	117	122	cm
FINISHED MEASUREMENTS						
Around bust						
41	43¼	45¼	47½	49½	52	in
104	110	115	121	126	132	cm
Length to shoulder						
24½	24¾	25	25½	26	26¼	in
62	63	64	65	66	67	cm

YARN

6 (7: 7: 8: 8: 9) x 1¾oz/186yd balls of Rowan *4-Ply Cotton* in Ripple 121

NEEDLES

Pair of size 1 (2.25mm) knitting needles
Pair of size 3 (3mm) knitting needles

20½ (21¾: 22¾: 23¾: 24¾: 26)in
52 (55: 57.5: 60.5: 63: 66)cm

24½ (24¾: 25: 25½: 26: 26¼)in
62 (63: 64: 65: 66: 67)cm

EXTRAS

7 buttons

GAUGE

29 sts and 38 rows to 4in/10cm measured over patt using size 3 (3mm) needles *or size to obtain correct gauge.*

ABBREVIATIONS

See page 132.

SPECIAL ABBREVIATION

M2 = make 2 sts by picking up, onto left needle, horizontal loop between needles and working [K1, P1] into back of this loop.

BACK
Left lower panel

Using size 1 (2.25mm) needles, cast on 36 (40: 44: 40: 44: 48) sts.
Row 1 (RS) *K1, P1; rep from * to end.
Row 2 *P1, K1; rep from * to end.
These 2 rows form seed st.
Work in seed st for 4 rows more.
Row 7 (RS) Seed st 2 sts, M2, seed st to end.
Work 5 rows.
Row 13 Rep row 7. 40 (44: 48: 44: 48: 52) sts.
Work 3 rows, ending with RS facing for next row.
Break off yarn and leave sts on a holder.

Center lower panel

Using size 1 (2.25mm) needles, cast on 65 (65: 65: 81: 81: 81) sts.
Row 1 (RS) K1, *P1, K1; rep from * to end.

Row 2 Rep row 1.

These 2 rows form seed st.

Work in seed st for 4 rows more.

Row 7 (RS) Seed st 2 sts, M2, seed st to last 2 sts, M2, seed st 2 sts.

Work 5 rows.

Row 13 Rep row 7. 73 (73: 73: 89: 89: 89) sts.

Work 3 rows, ending with RS facing for next row.

Break off yarn and leave sts on a holder.

Right lower panel

Using size 1 (2.25mm) needles, cast on 36 (40: 44: 40: 44: 48) sts.

Row 1 (RS) *P1, K1; rep from * to end.

Row 2 *K1, P1; rep from * to end.

These 2 rows form seed st.

Work in seed st for 4 rows more.

Row 7 (RS) Seed st to last 2 sts, M2, seed st 2 sts.

Work 5 rows.

Row 13 Rep row 7. 40 (44: 48: 44: 48: 52) sts.

Work 3 rows, ending with RS facing for next row.

Join panels

Row 17 (RS) Seed st first 39 (43: 47: 43: 47: 51) sts of Right Lower Panel, with WS of Center Lower Panel against RS of Right Lower Panel K tog first st of Center Lower Panel and last st of Right Lower Panel, seed st next 71 (71: 71: 87: 87: 87) sts of Center Lower Panel, with WS of Center Lower Panel against RS of Left Lower Panel K tog last st of Center Lower Panel and first st of Left Lower Panel, seed st rem 39 (43: 47: 43: 47: 51) sts of Left Lower Panel. 151 (159: 167: 175: 183: 191) sts.

Row 18 Purl.

Change to size 3 (3mm) needles.

Now work in patt as follows:

Row 1 (RS) K3 (7: 3: 7: 3: 7), P1, *K7, P1; rep from * to last 3 (7: 3: 7: 3: 7) sts, K3 (7: 3: 7: 3: 7).

Row 2 Purl.

These 2 rows form patt.

Counting in from both ends of last row, place markers on 40th (44th: 48th: 44th: 48th: 52nd) st in from both ends of row—there should be 71 (71: 71: 87: 87: 87) sts at center of row between marked sts.

Row 3 (RS) K2tog, [patt to within 2 sts of marked st, sl 1, K1, psso, K marked st, K2tog] twice, patt to last 2 sts, K2tog.

Work 15 rows.

Rep last 16 rows twice more, then row 3 again. 127 (135: 143: 151: 159: 167) sts.

Work 19 rows, ending with RS facing for next row.

Next row (RS) Inc in first st, [patt to marked st, M1, K marked st, M1] twice, patt to last st, inc in last st.

Work 13 rows.

Rep last 14 rows twice more, then first of these rows again. 151 (159: 167: 175: 183: 191) sts.

Work even in patt until Back measures 16 (16: 16½: 16½: 17: 17)in/41 (41: 42: 42: 43: 43)cm from cast-on edge, ending with RS facing for next row.

Shape armholes

Keeping patt correct, bind off 11 (12: 12: 13: 13: 14) sts at beg of next 2 rows. 129 (135: 143: 149: 157: 163) sts.

Dec 1 st at each end of next 11 (13: 13: 15: 15: 17) rows, then on foll 6 (6: 8: 8: 10: 10) alt rows, then on 4 foll 4th rows. 87 (89: 93: 95: 99: 101) sts.

Work even until armhole measures 8¼ (8½: 8½: 9: 9: 9½)in/21 (22: 22: 23: 23: 24)cm, ending with RS facing for next row.

Shape back neck and shoulders

Bind off 6 (7: 7: 7: 8: 8) sts at beg of next 2 rows. 75 (75: 79: 81: 83: 85) sts.

Next row (RS) Bind off 6 (7: 7: 7: 8: 8) sts, patt until there are 11 (10: 12: 12: 12: 13) sts on right needle and turn, leaving rem sts on a holder.

Work each side of neck separately.

Bind off 4 sts at beg of next row.

Bind off rem 7 (6: 8: 8: 8: 9) sts.

With RS facing, rejoin yarn to rem sts, bind off center 41 (41: 41: 43: 43: 43) sts, patt to end.

Complete to match first side, reversing shapings.

LEFT FRONT

Center lower panel

Using size 1 (2.25mm) needles, cast on 37 (37: 37: 45: 45: 45) sts.

Work in seed st as given for Lower Center Panel of Back for 6 rows.

Row 7 (RS) Seed st 2 sts, M2, seed st to end.

Work 5 rows.

Row 13 Rep row 7. 41 (41: 41: 49: 49: 49) sts.

Work 3 rows, ending with RS facing for next row.

Break off yarn and leave sts on a holder.

Left lower panel

Work as given for Right Lower Panel of Back.

Join panels

Row 17 (RS) Seed st first 39 (43: 47: 43: 47: 51) sts of Left Lower Panel, with WS of Center Lower Panel against RS of Left Lower Panel K tog first st of Center Lower Panel and last st of Left Lower Panel, seed st next 35 (35: 35: 43: 43: 43) sts of Center Lower Panel and turn, leaving rem 5 sts on a holder. 75 (79: 83: 87: 91: 95) sts.

Row 18 Purl.

Change to size 3 (3mm) needles.

Now work in patt as follows:

Row 1 (RS) K3 (7: 3: 7: 3: 7), *P1, K7; rep from * to end.

Row 2 Purl.

These 2 rows form patt.

Counting in from end of last row, place marker on 40th (44th: 48th: 44th: 48th: 52nd) st in from end of row—there should be 35 (35: 35: 43: 43: 43) sts beyond marked st.

Row 3 (RS) K2tog, patt to within 2 sts of marked st, sl 1, K1, psso, K marked st, K2tog, patt to end.

Work 15 rows.

Rep last 16 rows twice more, then row 3 again. 63 (67: 71: 75: 79: 83) sts.

Work 19 rows, ending with RS facing for next row.

Next row (RS) Inc in first st, patt to marked st, M1, K marked st, M1, patt to end.

Work 13 rows.

Rep last 14 rows twice more, then first of these rows again. 75 (79: 83: 87: 91: 95) sts.

Work even in patt until Left Front matches Back to start of armhole shaping, ending with RS facing for next row.

Shape armhole

Keeping patt correct, bind off 11 (12: 12: 13: 13: 14) sts

at beg of next row. 64 (67: 71: 74: 78: 81) sts.
Work 1 row.

Dec 1 st at armhole edge of next 11 (13: 13: 15: 15: 17) rows, then on foll 6 (6: 8: 8: 10: 10) alt rows, then on 1 (2: 1: 1: 0: 1) foll 4th rows. 46 (46: 49: 50: 53: 53) sts.

Work 2 (0: 0: 2: 2: 0) rows, ending with WS facing for next row.

Shape neck
Keeping patt correct, bind off 9 sts at beg of next row, then 4 sts at beg of foll alt row **and at the same time** dec 1 (0: 0: 1: 1: 0) st at armhole edge of 2nd of these rows. 32 (33: 36: 36: 39: 40) sts.

Dec 1 st at neck edge of next 5 rows, then on foll 3 (3: 3: 4: 4: 4) alt rows, then on 3 foll 4th rows **and at the same time** dec 1 st at armhole edge of 3rd (next: next: 3rd: 3rd: next) and 0 (1: 2: 1: 2: 2) foll 4th rows. 20 (20: 22: 22: 24: 25) sts.

Work even until Left Front matches Back to start of shoulder shaping, ending with RS facing for next row.

Shape shoulder
Bind off 6 (7: 7: 7: 8: 8) sts at beg of next row and foll alt row.
Work 1 row.
Bind off rem 8 (6: 8: 8: 8: 9) sts.

RIGHT FRONT
Right lower panel
Work as given for Left Lower Panel of Back.
Break off yarn and leave sts on a holder.

Center lower panel
Using size 1 (2.25mm) needles, cast on 37 (37: 37: 45: 45: 45) sts.

Work in seed st as given for Lower Center Panel of Back for 4 rows.

Row 5 (buttonhole row) (RS) Seed st 1 st, work 2 tog, [yo] twice (to make a buttonhole, drop extra loop on next row), seed st to end.
Work 1 row.

Row 7 (RS) Seed st to last 2 sts, M2, seed st 2 sts.
Work 5 rows.

Row 13 Rep row 7. 41 (41: 41: 49: 49: 49) sts.
Work 3 rows, ending with RS facing for next row.

Join panels
Row 17 (RS) Seed st first 5 sts of Center Lower Panel and slip these 5 sts onto a holder, seed st next 35 (35:

35: 43: 43: 43) sts of Center Lower Panel, with WS of Center Lower Panel against RS of Right Lower Panel, K tog last st of Center Lower Panel and first st of Right Lower Panel, seed st rem 39 (43: 47: 43: 47: 51) sts of Right Lower Panel. 75 (79: 83: 87: 91: 95) sts.

Row 18 Purl.
Change to size 3 (3mm) needles.
Now work in patt as follows:

Row 1 (RS) *K7, P1; rep from * to last 3 (7: 3: 7: 3: 7) sts, K3 (7: 3: 7: 3: 7).

Row 2 Purl.
These 2 rows form patt.

Counting in from beg of last row, place marker on 40th (44th: 48th: 44th: 48th: 52nd) st in from end of row—there should be 35 (35: 35: 43: 43: 43) sts beyond marked st.

Row 3 (RS) Patt to within 2 sts of marked st, sl 1, K1, psso, K marked st, K2tog, patt to last 2 sts, K2tog.
Complete to match Left Front, reversing shapings.

FINISHING
Press lightly on WS following instructions on yarn label.
Sew shoulder seams.

Button band
Slip 5 sts on left front holder onto size 1 (2.25mm) needles and rejoin yarn with RS facing.

Work in seed st as set until Button Band, when slightly stretched, fits up left front opening edge to neck shaping, ending with RS facing for next row.
Break off yarn and leave sts on a holder.

Slip stitch band in place. Mark positions for 7 buttons on this band—first to come level with buttonhole already made in Right Front, last to come just above neck shaping, and rem 5 buttons evenly spaced between.

Buttonhole band
Slip 5 sts on right front holder onto size 1 (2.25mm) needles and rejoin yarn with WS facing.

Work in seed st as set until Buttonhole Band, when slightly stretched, fits up right front opening edge to neck shaping, ending with RS facing for next row and with the addition of 5 more buttonholes worked to correspond with positions marked for buttons on Left Front as follows:

Buttonhole row (RS) Seed st 1 st, work 2 tog, [yo] twice (to make a buttonhole, drop extra loop on next row), seed st 2 sts.

When band is complete, do NOT break off yarn.

Slip stitch band in place.

Neckband

With RS facing and using size 1 (2.25mm) needles, seed st across 5 sts of Buttonhole Band, pick up and knit 63 (63: 63: 64: 64: 64) sts up right side of neck, 49 (49: 49: 51: 51: 51) sts from back, and 63 (63: 63: 64: 64: 64) sts down left side of neck, then seed st across 5 sts of Button Band. 185 (185: 185: 189: 189: 189) sts.

Keeping sts correct as set by bands, work in seed st across all sts as follows:

Work 1 row, ending with RS facing for next row.

Row 2 (RS) Seed st 1 st, work 2 tog, [yo] twice (to make 7th buttonhole, drop extra loop on next row), seed st to end.

Work in seed st for 3 rows more, ending with RS facing for next row.

Bind off in seed st.

Armhole borders (both alike)

With RS facing and using size 1 (2.25mm) needles, pick up and knit 143 (151: 151: 159: 159: 167) sts evenly all around armhole edge.

Work in seed st as given for Lower Center Panel of Back for 5 rows, ending with RS facing for next row.

Bind off in seed st.

Sew side and Armhole Border seams. Sew on buttons.

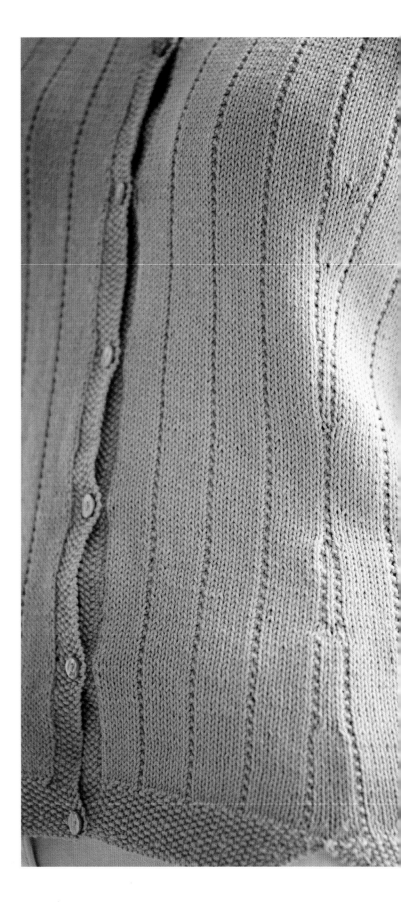

scarf and stole

JENNIE ATKINSON

SIZES

Scarf

The finished scarf measures 15in/38cm by 51in/130cm, excluding fringe.

Stole

The finished stole measures 23½in/60cm by 62in/157cm, excluding fringe.

(**Note:** The Scarf is shown on the opposite page and the Stole on pages 106 and 107.)

YARNS

Scarf

3 x ⁷/₈oz/229yd balls of Rowan *Kidsilk Haze* in Blushes 583

Stole

5 x ⁷/₈oz/229yd balls of Rowan *Kidsilk Haze* in Hurricane 632

NEEDLES

Pair of size 6 (4mm) knitting needles

EXTRAS

Scarf

Approximately 1,310 small silvered glass beads

Stole

Approximately 1,566 small silvered glass beads

GAUGE

24 sts and 32 rows to 4in/10cm measured over St st using size 6 (4mm) needles *or size to obtain correct gauge.*

ABBREVIATIONS

See page 132.

SPECIAL ABBREVIATION

bead 1 = place a bead by bringing yarn to front (RS) of work and slipping bead up next to stitch just worked, slip next stitch purlwise from left needle to right needle and take yarn back to back (WS) of work, leaving bead sitting in front of slipped stitch on RS of knitting.

BEADING NOTE

Before starting to knit, thread the beads onto the knitting yarn. To do this, thread a fine sewing needle (one that will easily pass through the beads) with a short length of sewing thread. Knot the ends of the thread together and then pass the end of the yarn throughthis loop. Thread a bead onto the sewing thread and then gently slide it along and onto the knitting yarn. Continue in this way until the required number of beads are on the yarn.

scarf

Thread half the beads onto yarn.

Using size 6 (4mm) needles, cast on 91 sts very loosely.

Row 1 (RS) Knit.

Row 2 and every foll alt row K3, P85, K3.

Row 3 K4, [K5, bead 1, K6] 7 times, K3.

Row 5 K4, [K4, bead 1, K1, bead 1, K5] 7 times, K3.

Row 7 K4, *[K3, bead 1] twice, K4; rep from * to last 3 sts, K3.

Row 9 K4, *[K2, bead 1] 3 times, K3; rep from * to last 3 sts, K3.

Row 11 K4, *[K1, bead 1, K2, bead 1] twice, K2; rep from * to last 3 sts, K3.

Row 13 K4, *bead 1, K2, [bead 1, K1] twice, bead 1, K2, bead 1, K1; rep from * to last 3 sts, K3.

Row 15 K3, bead 1, *K2, [bead 1, K1] 3 times, bead 1, K2, bead 1; rep from * to last 3 sts, K3.

Row 17 K4, *[K1, bead 1] 5 times, K2; rep from * to last 3 sts, K3.

Row 19 Rep row 15.

Row 21 Rep row 13.

Row 23 Rep row 11.

Row 25 Rep row 9.

Row 27 Rep row 7.

Row 29 Rep row 5.

Row 30 Rep row 2.

Rows 31–58 Rep rows 3–30.

Rows 59 and 60 Rep rows 3 and 4.

These 60 rows complete beaded border.

Break off yarn and remove beads.

Rejoin yarn and work lace section as follows:

Row 61 (RS) K4, *yo, sl 1, K1, psso, K1, K2tog, yo, K1; rep from * to last 3 sts, K3.

Row 62 and every foll alt row K3, P85, K3.

Row 63 K4, *yo, K1, sl 1, K2tog, psso, K1, yo, K1; rep from * to last 3 sts, K3.

Row 65 K4, *K2tog, yo, K1, yo, sl 1, K1, psso, K1; rep from * to last 3 sts, K3.

Row 67 K3, K2tog, *[K1, yo] twice, K1, sl 1, K2tog, psso; rep from * to last 8 sts, [K1, yo] twice, K1, sl 1, K1, psso, K3.

Row 69 K3, *K4, K2tog, yo, K1, yo, sl 1, K1, psso, K3; rep from * to last 4 sts, K4.

Row 70 Rep row 62.

Rep last 2 rows until Scarf measures 43in/109cm, ending with RS facing for next row.

Next row Rep row 65.

Next row Rep row 62.

Next row Rep row 67.

Next row Rep row 62.

Next row Rep row 61.

Next row Rep row 62.

Next row Rep row 63.

Next row Rep row 62.

Break off yarn and thread on rem beads.

Rejoin yarn and work second beaded border by repeating rows 3–60.

Bind off very loosely.

Press lightly on WS following instructions on yarn label and taking care not to damage beads.

Cut 300 lengths of yarn, each 15in/38cm long, and knot groups of 10 of these lengths through cast-on and bound-off edges to form fringe, positioning 15 knots evenly spaced along each end.

stole

Thread half the beads onto yarn.

Using size 6 (4mm) needles, cast on 143 sts very loosely.

(**Note:** Stole is shown on pages 106 and 107.)

Row 1 (RS) Knit.

Row 2 and every foll alt row K5, P133, K5.

Row 3 K6, [K5, bead 1, K6] 11 times, K5.

Row 5 K6, [K4, bead 1, K1, bead 1, K5] 11 times, K5.

Row 7 K6, *[K3, bead 1] twice, K4; rep from * to last 5 sts, K5.

Row 9 K6, *[K2, bead 1] 3 times, K3; rep from * to last 5 sts, K5.

Row 11 K6, *[K1, bead 1, K2, bead 1] twice, K2; rep from * to last 5 sts, K5.

Row 13 K6, *bead 1, K2, [bead 1, K1] twice, bead 1, K2, bead 1, K1; rep from * to last 5 sts, K5.

Row 15 K5, bead 1, *K2, [bead 1, K1] 3 times, bead 1, K2, bead 1; rep from * to last 5 sts, K5.

Row 17 K6, *[K1, bead 1] 5 times, K2; rep from * to last 5 sts, K5.

Row 19 Rep row 15.

Row 21 Rep row 13.

Row 23 Rep row 11.

Row 25 Rep row 9.

Row 27 Rep row 7.

Row 29 Rep row 5.

Row 31 Rep row 3.

Row 33 Rep row 5.

Row 35 K6, *K3, [bead 1, K1] twice, bead 1, K4; rep from * to last 5 sts, K5.

Row 37 K6, *K2, [bead 1, K1] 3 times, bead 1, K3; rep from * to last 5 sts, K5.

Row 39 Rep row 17.

Row 41 Rep row 37.

Row 43 Rep row 35.

Row 45 Rep row 5.

Row 47 Rep row 3.

Row 48 Rep row 2.

These 48 rows complete beaded border.

Break off yarn and remove beads.

Rejoin yarn and work lace section as follows:

Row 49 (RS) K6, *yo, sl 1, K1, psso, K1, K2tog, yo, K1; rep from * to last 5 sts, K5.

Row 50 and every foll alt row K5, P133, K5.

Row 51 K6, *yo, K1, sl 1, K2tog, psso, K1, yo, K1; rep from * to last 5 sts, K5.

Row 53 K6, *K2tog, yo, K1, yo, sl 1, K1, psso, K1; rep from * to last 5 sts, K5.

Row 55 K5, K2tog, *[K1, yo] twice, K1, sl 1, K2tog, psso; rep from * to last 10 sts, [K1, yo] twice, K1, sl 1, K1, psso, K5.

Row 57 K5, *K4, K2tog, yo, K1, yo, sl 1, K1, psso, K3; rep from * to last 6 sts, K6.

Row 58 Rep row 50.

Rep last 2 rows until Stole measures 55in/140cm, ending with RS facing for next row.

Next row Rep row 53.

Next and every foll alt row Rep row 50.

Next row Rep row 55.

Next row Rep row 49.

Next row Rep row 51.

Next row Rep row 50.

Break off yarn and thread on rem beads.

Rejoin yarn and work second beaded border as follows:

Work rows 31–46 as given for first beaded border, then work rows 3–32 as given for first beaded border.

Bind off very loosely.

FINISHING

Press lightly on WS following instructions on yarn label and taking care not to damage beads.

Cut 260 lengths of yarn, each 12in/30cm long, and knot groups of 10 of these lengths through cast-on and bound-off edges to form fringe, positioning 13 knots evenly spaced along each end.

camisole

JENNIE ATKINSON

TO FIT BUST

38	40	42	44	46	48	in
97	102	107	112	117	122	cm

FINISHED MEASUREMENTS

Around bust

33½	35¾	37¾	40	42½	45	in
85	91	96	102	108	114	cm

(**Note:** Garment is designed to be very close fitting and to hug body tightly.)

Length to shoulder, including strap

21½	22	22½	22¾	23¼	23½	in
55	56	57	58	59	60	cm

YARN

4 (4: 5: 5: 5: 6) x 1¾oz/186yd balls of Rowan *4-Ply Cotton* in Cream 153

NEEDLES

Pair of size 2 (2.75mm) knitting needles
Pair of size 3 (3mm) knitting needles

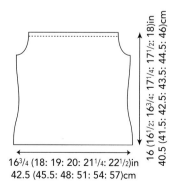

16¾ (18: 19: 20: 21¼: 22½)in
42.5 (45.5: 48: 51: 54: 57)cm

16 (16½: 16¾: 17¼: 17½: 18)in
40.5 (41.5: 42.5: 43.5: 44.5: 46)cm

GAUGE

28 sts and 38 rows to 4in/10cm measured over St st using size 3 (3mm) needles *or size to obtain correct gauge.*

ABBREVIATIONS

See page 132.

BACK

Using size 2 (2.75mm) needles, cast on 125 (133: 141: 149: 157: 165) sts.
Starting with a K row, work in St st for 7 rows, ending with WS facing for next row.
Change to size 3 (3mm) needles.
Row 8 (WS) Purl.
Row 9 (picot foldline row) K1, *yo, K2tog; rep from * to end.
Work in St st for 9 rows more, ending with RS facing for next row.
Now place vertical lacy lines as follows:
Row 1 (RS) K35 (37: 39: 41: 43: 45), yo, sl 1, K1, psso, K25 (27: 29: 31: 33: 35), yo, K2tog, K24 (26: 28: 30: 32: 34), K2tog, yo, K to end.
Row 2 and every foll alt row Purl.
Row 3 Rep row 1.
Row 5 K2tog, K34 (36: 38: 40: 42: 44), yo, sl 1, K1, psso, K24 (26: 28: 30: 32: 34), yo, K2tog, K23 (25: 27: 29: 31: 33), K2tog, yo, K to last 2 sts, K2tog. 123 (131: 139: 147: 155: 163) sts.
Row 7 K35 (37: 39: 41: 43: 45), yo, sl 1, K1, psso, K24 (26: 28: 30: 32: 34), yo, K2tog, K23 (25: 27: 29: 31: 33), K2tog, yo, K to end.
Row 9 K2tog, K34 (36: 38: 40: 42: 44), yo, sl 1, K1, psso,

K23 (25: 27: 29: 31: 33), yo, K2tog, K22 (24: 26: 28: 30: 32), K2tog, yo, K to last 2 sts, K2tog. 121 (129: 137: 145: 153: 161) sts.

Row 11 K35 (37: 39: 41: 43: 45), yo, sl 1, K1, psso, K23 (25: 27: 29: 31: 33), yo, K2tog, K22 (24: 26: 28: 30: 32), K2tog, yo, K to end.

Row 13 K2tog, K34 (36: 38: 40: 42: 44), yo, sl 1, K1, psso, K22 (24: 26: 28: 30: 32), yo, K2tog, K21 (23: 25: 27: 29: 31), K2tog, yo, K to last 2 sts, K2tog. 119 (127: 135: 143: 151: 159) sts.

Row 15 K35 (37: 39: 41: 43: 45), yo, sl 1, K1, psso, K22 (24: 26: 28: 30: 32), yo, K2tog, K21 (23: 25: 27: 29: 31), K2tog, yo, K to end.

Row 16 Purl.

Cont in this way, keeping central lacy line as set and moving side lacy lines one st closer to central line on next row and every foll 4th row **and at the same time** dec 1 st at each end of next row and every foll 4th row until 105 (113: 121: 129: 137: 145) sts rem. There should now be 16 (18: 20: 22: 24: 26) sts between side eyelet holes and central hole.

Now keeping all lacy lines in positions as set, work 7 rows, ending with RS facing for next row.

Now start to move side lacy lines out toward side seams as follows:

Row 49 (RS) Inc in first st, K32 (34: 36: 38: 40: 42), K2tog, yo, K17 (19: 21: 23: 25: 27), yo, K2tog, K16 (18: 20: 22: 24: 26), yo, sl 1, K1, psso, K to last st, inc in last st. 107 (115: 123: 131: 139: 147) sts.

Row 50 and every foll alt row Purl.

Row 51 K34 (36: 38: 40: 42: 44), K2tog, yo, K17 (19: 21: 23: 25: 27), yo, K2tog, K16 (18: 20: 22: 24: 26), yo, sl 1, K1, psso, K to end.

Row 53 K33 (35: 37: 39: 41: 43), K2tog, yo, K18 (20: 22: 24: 26: 28), yo, K2tog, K17 (19: 21: 23: 25: 27), yo, sl 1, K1, psso, K to end.

Row 55 Inc in first st, K32 (34: 36: 38: 40: 42), K2tog, yo, K18 (20: 22: 24: 26: 28), yo, K2tog, K17 (19: 21: 23: 25: 27), yo, sl 1, K1, psso, K to last st, inc in last st. 109 (117: 125: 133: 141: 149) sts.

Row 57 K33 (35: 37: 39: 41: 43), K2tog, yo, K19 (21: 23: 25: 27: 29), yo, K2tog, K18 (20: 22: 24: 26: 28), yo, sl 1, K1, psso, K to end.

Row 59 Rep row 57.

Row 60 Purl.

Cont in this way, keeping central lacy line as set and moving side lacy lines one st closer to side seams on next row and every foll 4th row **and at the same time** inc 1 st at each end of next row and every foll 6th row until there are 117 (125: 133: 141: 149: 157) sts. There should now be 24 (26: 28: 30: 32: 34) sts between side eyelet holes and central hole.

Row 80 (WS) Purl.

Row 81 K31 (33: 35: 37: 39: 41), K2tog, yo, K25 (27: 29: 31: 33: 35), yo, K2tog, K24 (26: 28: 30: 32: 34), yo, sl 1, K1, psso, K to end.

Rows 82 and 83 Rep rows 80 and 81.

Row 84 Purl.

Row 85 Inc in first st, K57 (61: 65: 69: 73: 77), yo, K2tog, K to last st, inc in last st. 119 (127: 135: 143: 151: 159) sts.

Last 2 rows complete side seam shaping and set the sts for rest of Back.

Work even until Back measures 13 (13: 13¼: 13¼: 13¾: 13¾)in/33 (33: 34: 34: 35: 35)cm from picot foldline row, ending with RS facing for next row.**

Shape armholes and work back medallion

Place markers either side of center 7 sts of last row.

Row 1 (RS) Bind off 6 (5: 7: 6: 8: 7) sts, K to first marker, slip marker onto right needle, K1, K2tog, yo, K1, yo, sl 1, K1, psso, K1, slip second marker onto right needle, K to end.

Row 2 Bind off 6 (5: 7: 6: 8: 7) sts, P to end. 107 (117: 121: 131: 135: 145) sts.

Row 3 K2tog, K to first marker, slip marker onto right needle, K2tog, yo, K3, yo, sl 1, K1, psso, slip second marker onto right needle, K to last 2 sts, K2tog.

Row 4 P2tog, P to last 2 sts, P2tog.

Row 5 K2tog, K to first marker, slip marker onto right needle, K2, yo, sl 1, K2tog, psso, yo, K2, slip second marker onto right needle, K to last 2 sts, K2tog.

Row 6 Rep row 4.

Row 7 K2tog, K to first marker, slip marker onto right needle, K3, yo, K2tog, K2, slip second marker onto right needle, K to last 2 sts, K2tog. 97 (107: 111: 121: 125: 135) sts.

Starting with a P row, work in St st for 10 (14: 14: 18: 18: 22) rows, dec 1 st at each end of every row and ending with WS facing for next row. 77 (79: 83: 85: 89: 91) sts.

Work in garter st for 4 rows, ending with WS facing for next row.

Bind off knitwise (on WS).

FRONT

Work as given for Back to **.

Shape armholes and work front medallion

Place markers either side of center 11 sts of last row.

Row 1 (RS) Bind off 3 (2: 4: 3: 5: 4) sts, K to first marker, slip marker onto right needle, K3, K2tog, yo, K1, yo, sl 1, K1, psso, K3, slip second marker onto right needle, K to end.

Row 2 Bind off 3 (2: 4: 3: 5: 4) sts, P to end. 113 (123: 127: 137: 141: 151) sts.

Row 3 K2tog, K to first marker, slip marker onto right needle, K2, K2tog, yo, K3, yo, sl 1, K1, psso, K2, slip second marker onto right needle, K to last 2 sts, K2tog.

Row 4 P2tog, P to last 2 sts, P2tog.

Row 5 K2tog, K to first marker, slip marker onto right needle, K1, [K2tog, yo] twice, K1, [yo, sl 1, K1, psso] twice, K1, slip second marker onto right needle, K to last 2 sts, K2tog.

Row 6 Rep row 4.

Row 7 K2tog, K to first marker, slip marker onto right needle, [K2tog, yo] twice, K3, [yo, sl 1, K1, psso] twice, slip second marker onto right needle, K to last 2 sts, K2tog.

Row 8 Rep row 4.

Row 9 K2tog, K to first marker, slip marker onto right needle, K1, [yo, sl 1, K1, psso] twice, K1, [K2tog, yo] twice, K1, slip second marker onto right needle, K to last 2 sts, K2tog. 99 (109: 113: 123: 127: 137) sts.

Row 10 Rep row 4.

Row 11 K2tog, K to first marker, slip marker onto right needle, K2, yo, sl 1, K1, psso, yo, sl 1, K2tog, psso, yo, K2tog, yo, K2, slip second marker onto right needle, K to last 2 sts, K2tog.

Row 12 Rep row 4.

Row 13 K2tog, K to first marker, slip marker onto right needle, K3, yo, sl 1, K1, psso, K1, K2tog, yo, K3, slip second marker onto right needle, K to last 2 sts, K2tog.

Row 14 Rep row 4.

Row 15 K2tog, K to first marker, slip marker onto right needle, K4, yo, sl 1, K2tog, psso, yo, K4, slip second marker onto right needle, K to last 2 sts, K2tog.
Row 16 Rep row 4.
Row 17 K2tog, K to first marker, slip marker onto right needle, K5, yo, K2tog, K4, slip second marker onto right needle, K to last 2 sts, K2tog. 83 (93: 97: 107: 111: 121) sts.
Row 18 [P2tog] 0 (1: 1: 1: 1: 1) times, P to last 0 (2: 2: 2: 2: 2) sts, [P2tog] 0 (1: 1: 1: 1: 1) times. 83 (91: 95: 105: 109: 119) sts.
Starting with a K row, work in St st, dec 1 st at each end of next 1 (3: 3: 7: 7: 11) rows, then on foll 2 (3: 3: 3: 3: 3) alt rows. 77 (79: 83: 85: 89: 91) sts.
Work 2 rows, ending with WS facing for next row.
Work in garter st for 4 rows, ending with WS facing for next row.
Bind off knitwise (on WS).

SHOULDER STRAPS (make 2)
Using size 2 (2.75mm) needles, cast on 11 sts.
Row 1 (RS) K1, [P1, K1] 5 times.
Row 2 P1, [K1, P1] 5 times.
Rep these 2 rows until Shoulder Strap measures 17¼ (18: 18: 19: 19: 19½)in/44 (46: 46: 48: 48: 50)cm from cast-on edge, ending with RS facing for next row.
Bind off.

FINISHING
Press lightly on WS following instructions on yarn label. Sew side seams. For front and back, fold first 8 rows to inside along picot foldline row and slip stitch in place. Sew together cast-on and bound-off ends of each Shoulder Strap to form a loop, then sew one edge to armhole edge, matching seams at underarm and stretching Shoulder Strap slightly to fit along shaped armhole row-end edges.

peplum jacket

JENNIE ATKINSON

TO FIT BUST

38	40	42	44	46	48	in
97	102	107	112	117	122	cm

FINISHED MEASUREMENTS

Around waist

36½	39¼	42	44½	47¼	50	in
93	100	107	113	120	127	cm

Length to shoulder (at side seam)

23¼	24	24	24¾	24¾	25	in
59	61	61	63	63	64	cm

(**Note:** Hemline is curved, so it is longer than "length to shoulder" at center back and shorter at center front.)

YARN

6 (6: 7: 7: 7: 8) x ⅞oz/229yd balls of Rowan *Kidsilk Haze* in Blackcurrant 641

NEEDLES

Pair of size 6 (4mm) knitting needles
Pair of size 10 (6mm) knitting needles
2 double-pointed size 6 (4mm) knitting needles

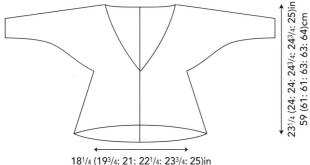

18¼ (19¾: 21: 22¼: 23¾: 25)in
46.5 (50: 53.5: 56.5: 60: 63.5)cm

23¼ (24: 24: 24¾: 24¾: 25)in
59 (61: 61: 63: 63: 64)cm

GAUGE

24 sts and 32 rows to 4in/10cm measured over patt using size 6 (4mm) needles *or size to obtain correct gauge.*

ABBREVIATIONS

See page 132.

RIGHT BACK

Using size 6 (4mm) needles, cast on 136 (140: 144: 148: 152: 156) sts.

Row 1 (RS) K12, yo, K2tog, K23 (24: 25: 26: 27: 28) placing marker on 12th (13th: 13th: 14th: 14th: 15th) of these sts, yo, K2tog, [K25 (26: 27: 28: 29: 30) placing marker on 13th (14th: 14th: 15th: 15th: 16th) of these sts, yo, K2tog] twice, K27 (28: 29: 30: 31: 32) placing marker on 14th (14th: 15th: 15th: 16th: 16th) of these sts, yo, K2tog, K14.

Row 2 Purl.

These 2 rows form patt—vertical lacy lines on a background of St st. (There should be 4 marked sts—one between each pair of vertical lacy lines.)

Work in patt for 8 rows more, ending with RS facing for next row.

Keeping vertical lacy lines correct as set, cont as follows:

Row 11 (RS) K1, K2tog, [patt to within 1 st of marked st, sl 1, K2tog (marked st is first of these 2 sts), psso] 4 times, patt to last 3 sts, sl 1, K1, psso, K1. 126 (130: 134: 138: 142: 146) sts.

Work 9 rows.

Rep last 10 rows 6 times more. 66 (70: 74: 78: 82: 86) sts. Remove marker nearest end of last row, leaving 3 marked sts in total.

Row 81 (RS) [Patt to within 1 st of marked st, sl 1, K2tog (marked st is first of these 2 sts), psso] 3 times, patt to last 3 sts, sl 1, K1, psso, K1. 59 (63: 67: 71: 75: 79) sts.

Row 82 Patt to last 4 sts and turn.

Row 83 Patt to end.

Row 84 Patt to last 8 sts and turn.

Row 85 Patt to end.

Row 86 Patt to last 12 sts and turn.

Row 87 Patt to end.

Row 88 Patt to last 16 sts and turn.

Row 89 Patt to end.

Row 90 Patt to last 20 sts and turn.

Remove "center" 2 markers, leaving the one nearest beg of last row.

Row 91 Patt to within 1 st of marked st, sl 1, K2tog (marked st is first of these 2 sts), psso, patt to last 3 sts, sl 1, K1, psso, K1.

Remove last marker—all decreases now complete. There should now be a total of 56 (60: 64: 68: 72: 76) sts.

Row 92 Patt to last 24 sts and turn.

Row 93 Patt to end.

Row 94 Patt to last 28 sts and turn.

Row 95 Patt to end.

Row 96 Patt to last 32 sts and turn.

Row 97 Patt to end.

KNITTING GOES LARGE

Cont in this way, working 4 fewer sts before turning on next row and every foll alt row, until the following row has been worked:

Next row (WS) Patt 4 sts and turn.

Next row Patt 4 sts.

Work 1 row across all sts.

Shape waist casing

Next row (RS) Knit.

Next row Knit.

Next row K2 (1: 5: 4: 3: 2), yo, K2tog, *K3, yo, K2tog; rep from * to last 2 sts, K2.

Next row Knit.

These 4 rows complete waist casing.

Now work in patt as follows:

Row 1 (RS) K5, yo, K2tog, *K9 (10: 11: 12: 13: 14), yo, K2tog; rep from * to last 5 sts, K5.

Row 2 Purl.

These 2 rows form patt for rest of Right Back.

Shape underarm and sleeve seam

Work in patt, inc 1 st at beg (side seam edge) of next row and at same edge on foll 43 rows, taking inc sts into patt and ending with RS facing for next row. 100 (104: 108: 112: 116: 120) sts.

Cast on 4 sts at beg of next row and foll 4 (4: 5: 5: 6: 6) alt rows, then 60 (64: 66: 70: 70: 74) sts at beg of foll alt row, taking cast-on sts into patt. 180 (188: 198: 206: 214: 222) sts.

Work even until work measures 5½ (6: 6: 6¼: 6¼: 6½)in/ 14 (15: 15: 16: 16: 17)cm from last set of cast-on sts, ending with WS facing for next row.

Using a size 10 (6mm) needle, purl 1 row.

Break off yarn and leave sts on a holder.

LEFT BACK

Using size 6 (4mm) needles, cast on 136 (140: 144: 148: 152: 156) sts.

Row 1 (RS) K15, yo, K2tog, K27 (28: 29: 30: 31: 32) placing marker on 14th (14th: 15th: 14th: 16th: 15th) of these sts, [yo, K2tog, K25 (26: 27: 28: 29: 30) placing marker on 13th (13th: 14th: 14th: 15th: 15th) of these sts] twice, yo, K2tog, K23 (24: 25: 26: 27: 28) placing marker on 12th (12th: 13th: 13th: 14th: 14th) of these sts, yo, K2tog, K11.

Row 2 Purl.

These 2 rows form patt—vertical lacy lines on a background of St st. (There should be 4 marked sts—one between each pair of vertical lacy lines.)

Work in patt for 8 rows more, ending with RS facing for next row.

Keeping vertical lacy lines correct as set, cont as follows:

Row 11 (RS) K1, K2tog, [patt to within 1 st of marked st, sl 1, K2tog (marked st is first of these 2 sts), psso] 4 times, patt to last 3 sts, sl 1, K1, psso, K1. 126 (130: 134: 138: 142: 146) sts.

Work 9 rows.

Rep last 10 rows 6 times more. 66 (70: 74: 78: 82: 86) sts. Remove marker nearest beg of last row, leaving 3 marked sts in total.

Row 81 (RS) K1, K2tog, [patt to within 1 st of marked st, sl 1, K2tog (marked st is first of these 2 sts), psso] 3 times, patt to end. 59 (63: 67: 71: 75: 79) sts.

Work 1 row.

Row 83 Patt to last 4 sts and turn.

Row 84 Patt to end.

Row 85 Patt to last 8 sts and turn.

Row 86 Patt to end.

Row 87 Patt to last 12 sts and turn.

Row 88 Patt to end.

Row 89 Patt to last 16 sts and turn.

Row 90 Patt to end.

Remove "center" 2 markers, leaving the one nearest end of last row.

Row 91 K1, K2tog, patt to within 1 st of marked st, sl 1, K2tog (marked st is first of these 2 sts), psso, patt to last 20 sts and turn.

Remove last marker—all decreases now complete. There should now be a total of 56 (60: 64: 68: 72: 76) sts.

Row 92 Patt to end.

Row 93 Patt to last 24 sts and turn.

Row 94 Patt to end.

Row 95 Patt to last 28 sts and turn.

Row 96 Patt to end.

Row 97 Patt to last 32 sts and turn.

Row 98 Patt to end.

Cont in this way, working 4 fewer sts before turning on next row and every foll alt row, until the following row has been worked:

Next row (RS) Patt 4 sts and turn.

Next row Patt 4 sts.

Shape waist casing

Next row (RS) Knit.

Next row Knit.

Next row K2, sl 1, K1, psso, yo, *K3, sl 1, K1, psso, yo; rep from * to last 2 (1: 5: 4: 3: 2) sts, K2 (1: 5: 4: 3: 2).

Next row Knit.

These 4 rows complete waist casing.

Now work in patt as follows:

Row 1 (RS) K5, yo, K2tog, *K9 (10: 11: 12: 13: 14), yo, K2tog; rep from * to last 5 sts, K5.

Row 2 Purl.

These 2 rows form patt for rest of Left Back.

Shape underarm and sleeve seam

Work in patt, inc 1 st at end (side seam edge) of next row and at same edge on foll 43 rows, taking inc sts into patt and ending with RS facing for next row. 100 (104: 108: 112: 116: 120) sts.

Work 1 row.

Cast on 4 sts at beg of next row and foll 4 (4: 5: 5: 6: 6) alt rows, then 60 (64: 66: 70: 70: 74) sts at beg of foll alt row, taking cast-on sts into patt. 180 (188: 198: 206: 214: 222) sts.

Work even until work measures 5½ (6: 6: 6¼: 6¼: 6½)in/ 14 (15: 15: 16: 16: 17)cm from last set of cast-on sts, ending with WS facing for next row.

Using a size 10 (6mm) needle, purl 1 row.

Break off yarn and leave sts on a holder.

RIGHT FRONT

Using size 6 (4mm) needles, cast on 105 (109: 113: 117: 121: 125) sts.

Row 1 (RS) K24 (25: 26: 27: 28: 29) placing marker on 15th (15th: 16th: 16th: 17th: 17th) of these sts, yo, K2tog, K19 (20: 21: 22: 23: 24) placing marker on 10th (10th: 11th: 11th: 12th: 12th) of these sts, yo, K2tog, [K21 (22: 23: 24: 25: 26) placing marker on 11th (11th: 12th: 12th: 13th: 13th) of these sts, yo, K2tog] twice, K12.

Row 2 P to last 5 sts, K5.

These 2 rows form patt—vertical lacy lines on a background of St st with front opening edge 5 sts in garter st. (There should be 4 marked sts—one between each pair of vertical lacy lines, and one between garter st front border and first vertical lacy line.)

Work in patt for 8 rows more, ending with RS facing for next row.

Keeping vertical lacy lines correct and 5 sts garter st at front opening edge as set, cont as follows:

Row 11 (RS) [Patt to within 1 st of marked st, sl 1, K2tog (marked st is first of these 2 sts), psso] 4 times, patt to last 3 sts, sl 1, K1, psso, K1. 96 (100: 104: 108: 112: 116) sts.

Work 9 rows.

Rep last 10 rows 3 times more, then row 11 again. 60 (64: 68: 72: 76: 80) sts.

Remove the 2 markers nearest front opening edge, leaving the 2 markers nearest side seam edge.

Work 6 rows, ending with WS facing for next row.

Row 58 (WS) Patt to last 9 sts and turn.

Row 59 Patt to end.

Row 60 Patt to last 13 sts and turn.

Row 61 [Patt to within 1 st of marked st, sl 1, K2tog (marked st is first of these 2 sts), psso] twice, patt to last 3 sts, sl 1, K1, psso, K1.

Remove last 2 markers—all decreases now complete. There should now be a total of 55 (59: 63: 67: 71: 75) sts.

Row 62 Patt to last 17 sts and turn.

Row 63 Patt to end.

Row 64 Patt to last 21 sts and turn.

Row 65 Patt to end.

Row 66 Patt to last 25 sts and turn.

Row 67 Patt to end.

Row 68 Patt to last 29 sts and turn.

Row 69 Patt to end.

Cont in this way, working 4 fewer sts before turning on next row and every foll alt row, until the following row has been worked:

Row 78 (WS) Patt 6 (10: 14: 18: 22: 26) sts and turn.

Work 2 rows across all sts.

Shape waist casing

Next row (RS) Knit.

Next row Knit.

Next row K8, yo, K2tog, *K3, yo, K2tog; rep from * to last 5 (4: 3: 2: 1: 5) sts, K5 (4: 3: 2: 1: 5).

Next row Knit.

These 4 rows complete waist casing.

Now work in patt as follows:

Row 1 (RS) K5, *K9 (10: 11: 12: 13: 14), yo, K2tog; rep from * to last 6 sts, K6.

Row 2 P to last 5 sts, K5.

These 2 rows form patt for rest of Right Front.

Shape front slope, and underarm and sleeve seam
Next row (RS) K5, K2tog (for front slope decrease), patt to last st, inc in last st (for side seam increase).
Inc 1 st at side seam edge of next 43 rows, taking inc sts into patt and ending with RS facing for next row, **and at the same time** dec 1 st at front slope of 4th row and every foll 4th row, working all front slope decreases as set. 88 (92: 96: 100: 104: 108) sts.
Cast on 4 sts at beg of 2nd row and foll 4 (4: 5: 5: 6: 6) alt rows, then 60 (64: 66: 70: 70: 74) sts at beg of foll alt row, taking cast-on sts into patt, **and at the same time** dec 1 st at front slope edge of next row and 2 (2: 1: 2: 1: 0) foll 4th rows, then on 0 (0: 1: 0: 1: 2) foll 6th rows. 165 (173: 183: 191: 199: 207) sts.
Dec 1 st at front slope edge only on 2nd (4th: 4th: 2nd: 2nd: 4th) row and 1 (0: 0: 0: 0: 0) foll 4th row, then on every foll 6th row until 158 (166: 176: 183: 191: 199) sts rem.
Work even until Right Front matches Backs to row worked on size 10 (6mm) needle, ending with WS facing for next row.
Next row (WS) Using a size 10 (6mm) needle, P to last 5 sts and slip these 153 (161: 171: 178: 186: 194) sts onto a holder, then using size 6 (4mm) needles, K5. Work in garter st on these rem 5 sts (for back neck border extension) for 4¼ (4¼: 4¼: 4½: 4½: 4½)in/ 11 (11: 11: 11.5: 11.5: 11.5)cm, ending with RS facing for next row.
Bind off.

LEFT FRONT
Using size 6 (4mm) needles, cast on 105 (109: 113: 117: 121: 125) sts.
Row 1 (RS) K13, [yo, K2tog, K21 (22: 23: 24: 25: 26) placing marker on 11th (12th: 12th: 13th: 13th: 14th) of these sts] twice, yo, K2tog, K19 (20: 21: 22: 23: 24) placing marker on 10th (11th: 11th: 12th: 12th: 13th) of these sts, yo, K2tog, K24 (25: 26: 27: 28: 29) placing marker on 10th (11th: 11th: 12th: 12th: 13th) of these sts.
Row 2 K5, P to end.
These 2 rows form patt—vertical lacy lines on a background of St st with front opening edge 5 sts in garter st. (There should be 4 marked sts—one between each pair of vertical lacy lines, and one between garter st front border and first vertical lacy line.)

Work in patt for 8 rows more, ending with RS facing for next row.
Keeping vertical lacy lines correct as set, cont as follows:
Row 11 (RS) K1, K2tog, [patt to within 1 st of marked st, sl 1, K2tog (marked st is first of these 2 sts), psso] 4 times, patt to end. 96 (100: 104: 108: 112: 116) sts.
Work 9 rows.
Rep last 10 rows 3 times more, then row 11 again. 60 (64: 68: 72: 76: 80) sts.
Remove the 2 markers nearest front opening edge, leaving the 2 markers nearest side seam edge.
Work 7 rows, ending with RS facing for next row.
Row 59 (RS) Patt to last 9 sts and turn.
Row 60 Patt to end.
Row 61 K1, K2tog, [patt to within 1 st of marked st, sl 1, K2tog (marked st is first of these 2 sts), psso] twice, patt to last 13 sts and turn.
Remove last 2 markers—all decreases now complete.
There should now be a total of 55 (59: 63: 67: 71: 75) sts.
Row 62 Patt to end.
Row 63 Patt to last 17 sts and turn.
Row 64 Patt to end.
Row 65 Patt to last 21 sts and turn.
Row 66 Patt to end.
Row 67 Patt to last 25 sts and turn.
Row 68 Patt to end.
Row 69 Patt to last 29 sts and turn.
Row 70 Patt to end.
Cont in this way, working 4 fewer sts before turning on next row and every foll alt row, until the following row has been worked:
Row 79 (RS) Patt 6 (10: 14: 18: 22: 26) sts and turn.
Work 1 row across all sts.
Shape waist casing
Next row (RS) Knit.
Next row Knit.
Next row K5 (4: 3: 2: 1: 5), sl 1, K1, psso, yo, *K3, sl 1, K1, psso, yo; rep from * to last 8 sts, K8.
Next row Knit.
These 4 rows complete waist casing.
Now work in patt as follows:
Row 1 (RS) K6, *yo, K2tog, K9 (10: 11: 12: 13: 14); rep from * to last 5 sts, K5.
Row 2 K5, P to end.

These 2 rows form patt for rest of Left Front.

Shape front slope, and underarm and sleeve seam

Next row (RS) Inc in first st (for side seam increase), patt to last 7 sts, sl 1, K1, psso (for front slope decrease), K5.
Inc 1 st at side seam edge of next 43 rows, taking inc sts into patt and ending with RS facing for next row, **and at the same time** dec 1 st at front slope of 4th row and every foll 4th row, working all front slope decreases as set. 88 (92: 96: 100: 104: 108) sts.

Cast on 4 sts at beg of next row and foll 4 (4: 5: 5: 6: 6) alt rows, then 60 (64: 66: 70: 70: 74) sts at beg of foll alt row, taking cast-on sts into patt, **and at the same time** dec 1 st at front slope edge of next row and 2 (2: 1: 2: 1: 0) foll 4th rows, then on 0 (0: 1: 0: 1: 2) foll 6th rows. 165 (173: 183: 191: 199: 207) sts.

Dec 1 st at front slope edge only on next (3rd: 3rd: next: next: 3rd) row and 1 (0: 0: 0: 0: 0) foll 4th row, then on every foll 6th row until 158 (166: 176: 183: 191: 199) sts rem.

Work even until Left Front matches Backs to row worked on size 10 (6mm) needle, ending with WS facing for next row.

Next row (WS) Using size 6 (4mm) needles, K5, then using a size 10 (6mm) needle, P to end and slip these 153 (161: 171: 178: 186: 194) sts onto a holder.
Break off yarn and rejoin it to rem 5 sts on needle.
Work in garter st on these rem 5 sts (for back neck border extension) for 4¼ (4¼: 4¼: 4½: 4½: 4½)in/ 11 (11: 11: 11.5: 11.5: 11.5)cm, ending with RS facing for next row.
Bind off.

FINISHING

Press lightly on WS following instructions on yarn label.

Join right overarm and shoulder seam

Holding RS of Right Front against RS of Right Back, rejoin yarn and using a size 10 (6mm) needle, bind off first st of Right Front with first st of Right Back, bind off rem 152 (160: 170: 177: 185: 193) sts of Right Front with corresponding sts of Right Back, then bind off rem 27 (27: 27: 28: 28: 28) sts of Right Back.

Join left overarm and shoulder seam

Holding RS of Left Back against RS of Left Front, rejoin yarn and using a size 10 (6mm) needle, bind off first st of Left Back with first st of Left Front, bind off rem 152 (160: 170: 177: 185: 193) sts of Left Back with corresponding sts of Left Front, then bind off rem 27 (27: 27: 28: 28: 28) sts of Left Back.

Sew center back seam. Sew side and underarm sleeve seams. Sew together bound-off edges of back neck border extensions, then sew one edge to back neck bound-off sts.

Tie

Using double-pointed size 6 (4mm) needles, cast on 4 sts.

Row 1 (RS) K4, without turning slip these 4 sts to opposite end of needle and bring yarn to opposite end of work pulling it quite tightly across WS of work ready to begin next row.
Rep row 1 until Tie is 72in/183cm long.
Bind off.
Thread Tie through eyelet holes of waist casing and tie ends at center front.

PEPLUM JACKET

twisted rib cardigan

WENDY BAKER

NEEDLES

Pair of size 6 (4mm) knitting needles
Cable needle

EXTRAS

1 large decorative pin (or kilt pin) for fastening (optional)

GAUGE

26 sts and 31 rows to 4in/10cm measured over patt using size 6 (4mm) needles *or size to obtain correct gauge.*

ABBREVIATIONS

See page 132.

TO FIT BUST

38	40	42	44	46	48	in
97	102	107	112	117	122	cm

FINISHED MEASUREMENTS

Around bust

47½	49¼	51	53	54¾	56½	in
121	125	130	135	139	144	cm

Length to shoulder

27	27½	28	28¼	28¾	29	in
69	70	71	72	73	74	cm

Sleeve seam

17½	17½	18	18	18	18	in
45	45	46	46	46	46	cm

YARN

17 (18: 19: 19: 20: 21) x 1¾oz/123yd balls of Rowan *Wool Cotton* in Elf 946

SPECIAL ABBREVIATION

C3B = slip next 2 sts onto cable needle and leave at back of work, K1, then K2 from cable needle.

BACK

Using size 6 (4mm) needles, cast on 157 (163: 169: 175: 181: 187) sts.

Row 1 (WS) K2 (5: 3: 1: 4: 2), P3, *K2, P3; rep from * to last 2 (5: 3: 1: 4: 2) sts, K2 (5: 3: 1: 4: 2).

Row 2 P2 (5: 3: 1: 4: 2), C3B, *P2, C3B; rep from * to last 2 (5: 3: 1: 4: 2) sts, P2 (5: 3: 1: 4: 2).

These 2 rows form patt.

Work even in patt until Back measures 18½ (18½: 19: 19: 19¼: 19¼)in/47 (47: 48: 48: 49: 49)cm from cast-on edge, ending with RS facing for next row.

Shape armholes

Keeping patt correct, bind off 5 sts at beg of next 2 rows. 147 (153: 159: 165: 171: 177) sts.

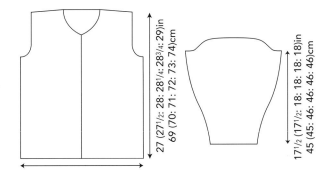

23¾ (24¾: 25½: 26½: 27½: 28¼)in
60.5 (62.5: 65: 67.5: 69.5: 72)cm

27 (27½: 28: 28¼: 28¾: 29)in
69 (70: 71: 72: 73: 74)cm

17½ (17½: 18: 18: 18: 18)in
45 (45: 46: 46: 46: 46)cm

Dec 1 st at each end of next row and foll 9 alt rows. 127 (133: 139: 145: 151: 157) sts.

Work even until armhole measures 8½ (9: 9: 9½: 9½: 9¾)in/22 (23: 23: 24: 24: 25)cm, ending with RS facing for next row.

Shape shoulders

Bind off 13 (14: 15: 16: 17: 18) sts at beg of next 4 rows, then 14 (15: 16: 16: 17: 18) sts at beg of foll 2 rows. Bind off rem 47 (47: 47: 49: 49: 49) sts.

LEFT FRONT

Using size 6 (4mm) needles, cast on 97 (100: 103: 106: 109: 112) sts.

Row 1 (WS) *K2, P3; rep from * to last 2 (5: 3: 1: 4: 2) sts, K2 (5: 3: 1: 4: 2).

Row 2 P2 (5: 3: 1: 4: 2), C3B, *P2, C3B; rep from * to last 2 sts, P2. These 2 rows form patt.

Work even in patt until Left Front matches Back to start of armhole shaping, ending with RS facing for next row.

Shape armhole

Keeping patt correct, bind off 5 sts at beg of next 2 rows. 92 (95: 98: 101: 104: 107) sts.

Work 1 row.

Dec 1 st at armhole edge of next row and foll 9 alt rows. 82 (85: 88: 91: 94: 97) sts.

Work even until 23 rows fewer have been worked than on Back to start of shoulder shaping, ending with WS facing for next row.

Shape neck

Keeping patt correct, bind off 3 (3: 3: 4: 4: 4) sts at beg of next row, then 3 sts at beg of foll 11 alt rows, ending with RS facing for next row. 46 (49: 52: 54: 57: 60) sts.

Shape shoulder

Bind off 13 (14: 15: 16: 17: 18) sts at beg of next row, then 3 sts at beg of foll row.
Rep last 2 rows once more.
Bind off rem 14 (15: 16: 16: 17: 18) sts.

RIGHT FRONT

Using size 6 (4mm) needles, cast on 97 (100: 103: 106: 109: 112) sts.
Row 1 (WS) K2 (5: 3: 1: 4: 2), P3, *K2, P3; rep from * to last 2 sts, K2.
Row 2 *P2, C3B; rep from * to last 2 (5: 3: 1: 4: 2) sts, P2 (5: 3: 1: 4: 2).
These 2 rows form patt.
Complete to match Left Front, reversing shapings.

SLEEVES (make 2)

Using size 6 (4mm) needles, cast on 72 (72: 74: 76: 76: 78) sts.
Row 1 (WS) P0 (0: 1: 2: 2: 3), *K2, P3; rep from * to last 2 (2: 3: 4: 4: 5) sts, K2, P0 (0: 1: 2: 2: 3).
Row 2 K0 (0: 1: 2: 2: 3), *P2, C3B; rep from * to last 2 (2: 3: 4: 4: 5) sts, P2, K0 (0: 1: 2: 2: 3).
These 2 rows form patt.
Work in patt until Sleeve measures 2in/5cm, ending with RS facing for next row.
Inc 1 st at each end of next row and every foll 4th row to 110 (122: 114: 122: 122: 130) sts, then on every foll 6th row until there are 122 (126: 126: 130: 130: 134) sts, taking inc sts into patt.
Work even until Sleeve measures 17½ (17½: 18: 18: 18: 18)in/45 (45: 46: 46: 46: 46)cm from cast-on edge, ending with RS facing for next row.
Shape top of sleeve
Keeping patt correct, bind off 5 sts at beg of next 2 rows. 112 (116: 116: 120: 120: 124) sts.
Dec 1 st at each end of next row and foll 8 alt rows, then on foll row, ending with RS facing for next row.
Bind off rem 92 (96: 96: 100: 100: 104) sts.

FINISHING

Press lightly on WS following instructions on yarn label.
Sew shoulder seams.
Collar
With RS facing and using size 6 (4mm) needles, starting and ending at front opening edges, pick up and knit 48 (48: 48: 49: 49: 49) sts up right side of neck, 50 (50: 50: 50: 52: 52: 52) sts from back, then 48 (48: 48: 49: 49: 49) sts down left side of neck. 146 (146: 146: 150: 150: 150) sts.
Row 1 (RS of Collar, WS of body) K10, *inc in next st, K1, P2; rep from * to last 12 sts, inc in next st, K11. 178 (178: 178: 183: 183: 183) sts.
Row 2 Bind off 8 sts knitwise (one st on right needle after bind-off), K1, *P3, K2; rep from * to last 8 sts, K8.
Row 3 Bind off 8 sts knitwise (one st on right needle after bind-off), K1, *C3B, P2; rep from * to last 5 sts, C3B, K2. 162 (162: 162: 167: 167: 167) sts.
Row 4 K2, *P3, K2; rep from * to end.
Row 5 K2, *C3B, P2; rep from * to last 5 sts, C3B, K2.
Rep last 2 rows until Collar measures 7in/18cm from pick-up row, ending with WS of Collar facing for next row.
Bind off in patt.
Sew sleeves into armholes. Sew side and sleeve seams.
Fasten fronts with decorative pin if desired.

cabled bag

SHARON BRANT

SIZE
The finished bag measures 15½in/39cm wide at base by 13¾in/35cm tall.

YARN
3 x 3½oz/186yd balls of Rowan *Scottish Tweed Aran* in Porridge 024

NEEDLES
Pair of size 8 (5mm) knitting needles
Cable needle

EXTRAS
Piece of ultra firm sew-in interfacing, to insert inside bottom of bag (optional)

GAUGE
16 sts and 24 rows to 4in/10cm measured over St st using size 8 (5mm) needles *or size to obtain correct gauge.*

ABBREVIATIONS
See page 132.

SPECIAL ABBREVIATION
C10F = slip next 5 sts onto cable needle and leave at front of work, K5, then K5 from cable needle.

FRONT OF BAG
Using size 8 (5mm) needles, cast on 84 sts.
Note: The bag is worked in alternating vertical panels of St st cables and seed stitch, and markers are used to situate the beginning and end of each vertical panel.

Row 1 (RS) K1, [P1, K1] 6 times, place marker on right needle, *K10 for cable panel, place marker on right needle, [P1, K1] 7 times, place marker on right needle; rep from * once, K10 for cable panel, place marker on right needle, [K1, P1] 6 times, K1.
Row 2 K1, [P1, K1] 6 times, slip marker onto right needle, *P10 for cable panel, slip marker onto right needle, [P1, K1] 7 times, slip marker onto right needle; rep from * once, P10 for cable panel, slip marker onto right needle, [K1, P1] 6 times, K1.
These 2 rows set seed stitch and cable panels.
Slipping markers when reached and keeping seed st and cable panels correct as set, cont as follows:
Row 3 Seed st 13 sts, *K10, seed st 14 sts; rep from * once, K10, seed st 13 sts.
Row 4 Seed st 13 sts, *P10, seed st 14 sts; rep from * once, P10, seed st 13 sts.

Shape sides
Beg cables and shaping (at each side of each cable, within seed st panels) on next row as follows:
Row 5 Seed st to last 2 sts of first seed st panel, work 2 sts tog, *C10F across cable panel sts, work 2 sts tog, seed st to last 2 sts of this seed st panel, work 2 sts tog; rep from * once, C10F across cable panel, work 2 sts tog, seed st to end.
**Row 6 Rep row 4.
Rows 7–14 [Rep rows 3 and 4] 4 times.
Row 15 Rep row 5.** 72 sts.
Rep from ** to ** 5 times more. 42 sts.
Next row Rep row 4.
Next row Rep row 3.
Rep last 2 rows once more, ending with WS facing for next row.

Top border

Knit 3 rows.

Beg with a K row, work 8 rows in St st, ending with RS facing for next row.

Work holes for handles on next 2 rows as follows:

Next row (RS) P8, bind off 6 sts, P until there are 14 sts on needle after last bind-off, bind off 6 sts, P to end (this row forms hem foldline).

Next row Purl to end, casting on 6 sts over each group of 6 sts bound off on previous row.

Beg with a K row, work 8 rows in St st.
Bind off.

BACK OF BAG

Work exactly as for Front.

GUSSET

Using size 8 (5mm) needles, cast on 20 sts.

Row 1 *K1, P1; rep from * to end.

Row 2 P1, K1; rep from * to end.

These 2 rows form seed st.

Work in seed st until Gusset is same length as cast-on edge of Front—this completes gusset at base of bag.

Shape first side panel of gusset

Mark each end of last row.

Next row (RS) Purl (to form a ridge at beg of side panel of gusset).

Beg with a P row, work in St st, dec 1 st at each end of 4th row and then every foll 6th row until 4 sts rem.

Work even until Gusset measures from marker same as side edge of Front to top of cabled section, ending with WS facing for next row.

Knit 3 rows.
Bind off.

Shape second side panel of gusset

With RS facing and using size 8 (5mm) needles, pick up and knit 20 sts along cast-on edge of gusset.

Next row (RS) Knit (to form a ridge at beg of side panel of gusset).

Beg with a K row, work in St st, dec 1 st at each end of 5th row and then every foll 6th row until 4 sts rem.

Work even until Gusset measures from pick-up row same as side edge of Front to top of cabled section, ending with WS facing for next row.

Knit 3 rows. Bind off.

HANDLES (make 2)

Using size 8 (5mm) needles, cast on 70 sts.
Knit 4 rows.
Bind off knitwise.

FINISHING

Sew one side edge of Gusset to Front along two side edges and cast-on edge of Front, beginning and ending at top of garter st section at beg of border on Front. Then sew other side edge of Gusset to Back in same way. Insert about 3cm/1¼in of end of one Handle from RS to WS through a hole in hem on Front of bag, then slip stitch both sides of end of Handle to WS of top border. Insert other end of this Handle through other hole and stitch in place in same way.

Stitch second Handle to Back of bag in same way.

Fold hems on Front and Back to WS along foldline (level with holes) and slip stitch in place.

If desired, cut a piece of ultra firm sew-in interfacing the same size as the bottom of the gusset (from cast-on edge to marker) and stitch in place inside bottom of bag.

CABLED BAG

knitting information

The following notes will help you produce successful knitted garments.

GAUGE

Obtaining the correct gauge can make the difference between a garment that fits and one that does not. It controls both the shape and size of a knitted garment, so any variation, however slight, can distort the finished size. Different designers feature in this book and it is their gauge, given at the start of each pattern, that you must match. To check this against your own gauge, knit a square in pattern and/or stockinette stitch (depending on the pattern instructions) of about 5 to 10 more stitches and 5 to 10 more rows than those given in the gauge note. Mark a central 4in (10cm) square with pins. If you have too many stitches to 4in (10cm), try again using a larger needle size. If you have too few stitches to 4in (10cm), try again using a smaller needle size.

Once you have achieved the correct gauge, your garment will be knitted to the measurements indicated in the size diagram shown with the pattern.

GARMENT SIZES AND SIZE DIAGRAMS

The instructions in each garment pattern are given for the smallest size. The figures in parentheses are for the larger sizes. Where there is one set of figures only, it applies to all sizes.

All garment patterns include "ease" to allow for a comfortable fit. The finished measurement around the bust of the knitted garment is given at the start of each pattern and includes this ease. The size diagram shows the finished width of the garment at the underarm, and it is this measurement that you should use to choose an appropriate size.

A useful tip is to measure one of your own garments that fits comfortably and choose a size that is similar. Having chosen a size based on width, look at the corresponding length for that size; if you are not happy with the total length that we recommend, adjust your

own garment before beginning your armhole shaping—any adjustment after this point will mean that your sleeve will not fit into your garment easily; and don't forget to take your adjustment into account if there is any side-seam shaping.

Finally, look at the sleeve length; the size diagram shows the finished sleeve measurement, taking into account any top-arm insertion length. Measure your body between the center of your neck and your wrist, this measurement should correspond to half the garment width plus the sleeve length. Again, your sleeve length may be adjusted, but remember to take into consideration the position of the sleeve increases if you do adjust the length. (See pages 6–13 for more about making alterations.)

KNITTING CHARTS

Two of the patterns in the book have charts as part of the instructions. Each square on a knitting chart represents a stitch and each line of squares represents a row of knitting. The key with the chart explains the symbols used on the chart.

When working from the charts, read odd-numbered rows (K) from right to left and even-numbered rows (P) from left to right, unless stated otherwise.

COLORWORK KNITTING

There are two main methods of working color into a knitted fabric: the intarsia and Fair Isle techniques. The first method produces a single thickness of fabric and is usually used where a color is only required in a particular area of a row. Where a repeating pattern is created across the row, the Fair Isle technique is usually used.

Intarsia technique

For this technique, cut lengths of yarn for each motif or block of color used in a row. Then join in the various colors at the appropriate position in the row, linking one color to the next by twisting them around each other where they meet on the wrong side to avoid gaps.

All yarn ends can then either be darned along the color join lines after each motif is completed, or can be "knitted-in" on the wrong side of the knitting as each color is worked into the pattern. This is done in much the same way as "weaving-in" yarns when working the Fair Isle technique and saves time darning-in ends.

It is essential that the gauge is noted for colorwork, because this may vary from the plain stockinette stitch gauge if both are used in the same pattern.

Fair Isle technique

When two or three colors are worked repeatedly across a row, strand the yarn not in use loosely behind the stitches being worked. If you are working with more than two colors, treat the "floating" yarns as if they were one yarn and always spread the stitches to their correct width to keep them elastic.

It is advisable not to carry the stranded or 'floating" yarns over more than three stitches at a time, but to weave them under and over the color you are working to catch the "floating" yarns into the back of the work.

SLIP-STITCH EDGINGS

When a row end edge forms the actual finished edge of a garment or an accessory like a scarf, a slip-stitch edging makes a neat edge.

To work a slip-stitch edging at the end of a right-side row, work across the row until there is one stitch left on the left needle. Pick up the loop lying between the needles and place this loop on the right needle. (Note that this loop does NOT count as a stitch and is not included in any stitch counts.) Now slip the last stitch knitwise with the yarn at the back of the work. At the beginning of the next row, purl together the first (slipped) stitch with the picked-up loop.

To work a slip-stitch edging at the end of a wrong-side row, work across the row until there is one stitch left on the left needle. Pick up the loop lying between the needles and place this loop on the right needle. (Note that this loop does NOT count as a stitch and is not included in any stitch counts.) Now slip the last stitch purlwise with the yarn at the front of the work. At the beginning of the next row, knit together through the back of the loop the first (slipped) stitch with the picked-up loop.

FINISHING INSTRUCTIONS

Follow these finishing tips for a truly professional-looking garment or accessory.

Blocking and pressing

Block out each piece of knitting by pinning it to the correct size on a padded surface. Following the instructions on the yarn label and avoiding any ribbing, press the pieces.

Take special care to press the edges, as this will make sewing the seams both easier and neater. If the yarn label indicates that the fabric should not be pressed, then covering the blocked out fabric with a damp white cotton cloth and leaving it to dry will have the desired effect.

Darn in all ends neatly along the selvage edge or a color join, as appropriate.

Sewing seams

When sewing the pieces together, remember to match areas of color and texture very carefully where they meet. Use backstitch or mattress stitch for all main knitting seams, and sew together ribbing and neckband seams with mattress stitch, unless stated otherwise.

Having completed the garment pieces, sew the seams in the order stated in the instructions. After sewing the shoulder seams, sew the top of the sleeve to the body of the garment using the method detailed in the pattern, referring to the appropriate guide:

Straight bound-off sleeves Place the center of the bound-off edge of the sleeve at the shoulder seam. Sew the top of the sleeve to the back and front.

Square set-in sleeves Place the center of the bound-off edge of the sleeve at the shoulder seam. Sew the top of the sleeve into the armhole, with the straight sides at the top of the sleeve forming a neat right-angle to the bound-off stitches at the armhole.

Shallow set-in sleeves Place the center of the bound-off edge of the sleeve at the shoulder seam. Match the decreases at the beginning of the armhole shaping with the decreases at the top of the sleeve, and sew the sleeve head to the armhole, easing in the shapings.

Set-in sleeves Place the center of the bound-off edge of the sleeve at the shoulder seam. Sew in the sleeve, easing the sleeve head into the armhole.

Lastly, slip stitch any pocket edgings and linings in place and sew on buttons to correspond with buttonholes.

knitting abbreviations

KNITTING ABBREVIATIONS

The following are the standard knitting abbreviations used in this book. Any special abbreviations (such as those for cables or beading) are given at the beginning of individual patterns.

alt	alternate
beg	begin(ning)
cm	centimeter(s)
cont	continu(e)(ing)
dec	decreas(e)(ing)
DK	double knitting (a lightweight yarn)
foll	follow(s)(ing)
g	gram(s)
garter st	garter stitch (K every row)
in	inch(es)
inc	increas(e)(ing)
inc 1	increase one st by working into front and back of stitch
K	knit
K2tog	knit next 2 sts together
m	meter(s)
M1	make one stitch by picking up horizontal loop before next stitch and knitting into back of it
MC	main color (of yarn)
mm	millimeter(s)
oz	ounce(s)
P	purl
P2tog	purl next 2 sts together

patt	pattern; or work in pattern
psso	pass slipped stitch over
rem	remain(s)(ing)
rep	repeat(s)(ing)
rev St st	reverse stockinette stitch (P all RS rows and K all WS rows)
RS	right side
sl	slip
st(s)	stitch(es)
St st	stockinette stitch (K all RS rows and P all WS rows)
tbl	through back of loop(s)
tog	together
WS	wrong side
yd	yard(s)
yo	yarn over right needle to make a new stitch

0	no stitches, times, or rows for that size
–	instructions do not apply to this size
*	Repeat instructions after asterisk or between asterisks as many times as instructed.
[ ]	Repeat instructions inside brackets as many times as instructed.

The following are the specifications of the Rowan yarns used for the designs in this book (see page 134 for yarn weight symbols). It is always best to try to obtain the exact yarns specified in the patterns. If, however, you wish to find a substitute yarn, use the yarn descriptions given below to find a similar yarn type and yarn weight. When substituting yarn, remember to calculate the yarn amount needed by yardage/meterage rather than by ball weight.

For yarn care directions, refer to the yarn label.

Rowan Classic Baby Alpaca DK

A lightweight alpaca yarn; 100 percent baby alpaca; 1³/₄oz/50g (approximately 109yd/100m) per ball; recommended gauge—22 sts and 30 rows to 4in/10cm measured over St st using size 6 (4mm) knitting needles.

Rowan Classic Cashsoft 4-Ply

A super-fine-weight wool-and-cashmere-mix yarn; 57 percent fine merino wool, 33 percent microfiber, 10 percent cashmere; 1³/₄oz/50g (approximately 197yd/180m) per ball; recommended gauge—28 sts and 36 rows to 4in/10cm measured over St st using size 3 (3.25mm) knitting needles.

Rowan Classic Silk Wool DK

A lightweight wool-and-silk-mix yarn; 50 percent silk, 50 percent merino wool; 1³/₄oz/50g (approximately 109yd/100m) per ball; recommended gauge—22 sts and 30 rows to 4in/10cm measured over St st using size 6 (4mm) knitting needles.

Rowan Cotton Glace

A fine-weight cotton yarn; 100 percent cotton; 1³/₄oz/50g (approximately 126yd/115m) per ball; recommended gauge—23 sts and 32 rows to 4in/10cm measured over St st using size 3–5 (3.25–3.75mm) knitting needles.

Rowan Denim

A lightweight cotton yarn; 100 percent cotton; 1³/₄oz/50g (approximately 102yd/93m) per ball; recommended gauge—20 sts and 28 rows (before washing) and 20 sts and 32 rows (after washing) to 4in/10cm measured over St st using size 6 (4mm) knitting needles.

Rowan 4-Ply Cotton

A super-fine-weight cotton yarn; 100 percent cotton; 1³/₄oz/50g (approximately 186yd/170m) per ball; recommended gauge—27–29 sts and 37–39 rows to 4in/10cm measured over St st using size 3 (3mm) knitting needles.

Rowan Kidsilk Haze

A fine-weight mohair-mix yarn; 70 percent super kid mohair, 30 percent silk; 25g/⁷/₈oz (approximately 229yd/210m) per ball; recommended gauge—18–25 sts and 23–34 rows to 4in/10cm measured over St st using 3.25–5mm (US sizes 3–8) knitting needles.

Rowan Scottish Tweed Aran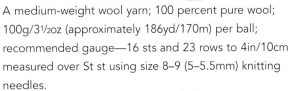

A medium-weight wool yarn; 100 percent pure wool; 100g/3¹/₂oz (approximately 186yd/170m) per ball; recommended gauge—16 sts and 23 rows to 4in/10cm measured over St st using size 8–9 (5–5.5mm) knitting needles.

Rowan Scottish Tweed DK

A lightweight wool yarn; 100 percent pure wool; 1³/₄oz/50g (approximately 123yd/113m) per ball; recommended gauge—20–22 sts and 28–30 rows to 4in/10cm measured over St st using size 6 (4mm) knitting needles.

Rowan Wool Cotton

A lightweight wool/cotton blend yarn; 50 percent merino wool, 50 percent cotton; 1³/₄oz/50g (approximately 123yd/113m) per ball; recommended gauge—22–24 sts and 30–32 rows to 4in/10cm measured over St st using size 5–6 (3.75–4mm) knitting needles.

Categories of yarn, gauge ranges, and recommended knitting needle sizes from the Craft Yarn Council of America.
YarnStandards.com

Yarn-weight symbol and category names	(0) LACE	(1) SUPER FINE	(2) FINE	(3) LIGHT	(4) MEDIUM	(5) BULKY	(6) SUPER BULKY
Types of yarns** in category	10-count crochet thread, fingering	4-ply, sock, fingering, baby	sport, baby	DK, light worsted	worsted, afghan, Aran	chunky, craft, rug	bulky, roving
Knit gauge ranges* in St st to 4in (10cm)	33–40*** sts	27–32 sts	23–26 sts	21–24 sts	16–20 sts	12–15 sts	6–11 sts
Recommended needle in metric size range	1.5–2.25 mm	2.25–3.25 mm	3.25–3.75 mm	3.7.5–4.5 mm	4.5–5.5 mm	6.5–8 mm	8mm and larger
Recommended needle in US size range	000 to 1	1 to 3	3 to 5	5 to 7	7 to 9	9 to 11	11 and larger

* **GUIDELINES ONLY** The above reflect the most commonly used gauges and needle sizes for specific yarn categories.

** The generic yarn-weight names in the yarn categories include those commonly used in the US and UK.

*** Ultra-fine lace-weight yarns are difficult to put into gauge ranges; always follow the gauge given in your pattern for these yarns.

ROWAN YARN ADDRESSES

Contact the distributors listed here to find a supplier of Rowan hand knitting yarns near you. For countries not listed, contact the main office in the UK or the Rowan websites:
www.knitrowan.com
www.rowanclassic.com

USA
Westminster Fibers Inc.,
165 Ledge Street, Nashua,
NH 03060.
Tel: 1-800-445-9276.
E-mail: rowan@westminsterfibers.com
www.westminsterfibers.com

AUSTRALIA
Australian Country Spinners,
314 Albert Street, Brunswick,
Victoria 3056. Tel: (61) 3 9380 3888.
Fax: (61) 3 9387 2674.
E-mail: sales@auspinners.com.au

AUSTRIA
Coats Harlander GmbH,
Autokaderstrasse 31, A-1230 Wien.
Tel: (01) 27716-0.
Fax: (01) 27716-228.

BELGIUM
Coats Benelux, Ring Oost 14A,
Ninove, 9400. Tel: 0346 35 37 00.
E-mail: sales.coatsninove@coats.com

CANADA
Same as USA.

CHINA
Coats Shanghai Ltd., No. 9 Building,
Boasheng Road, Songjiang Industrial
Zone, Shanghai, 201613.
Tel: (86-21) 5774 3733.
Fax: (86-21) 5774 3768.

DENMARK
Coats HP A/S, Nannagade 28,
2200 Kobenhavn N.
Tel: 35 86 90 50. Fax: 35 82 15 10.
E-mail: info@hpgruppen.dk
www.hpgruppen.dk

FINLAND
Coats Opti Oy, Ketjutie 3,
04220 Kerava. Tel: (358) 9 274 871.
Fax: (358) 9 2748 7330.
E-mail: coatsopti.sales@coats.com

FRANCE
Coats France/Steiner Fréres,
SAS 100 avenue du Général de
Gaulle, 18 500 Mehun-Sur-Yèvre.
Tel: 02 48 23 12 30.
Fax: 02 48 23 12 40.

GERMANY
Coats GMbH, Kaiserstrasse 1,
D-79341 Kenzingen.
Tel: 7644 8020. Fax: 7644 802399.
www.coatsgmbh.de

HOLLAND
Same as Belgium.

HONG KONG
Coats China Holding Ltd.,
19/F Millenium City 2, 378 Kwun
Tong Road, Kwun Tong, Kowloon.
Tel: (852) 2798 6886.
Fax: (852) 2305 0311.

ICELAND
Storkurinn, Laugavegi 59,
101 Reykjavek. Tel: (354) 551 8258.
E-mail: storkurinn@simnet.is

ITALY
Coats Cucirini srl, Via Sarca 223,
20126 Milano.
Tel: 800 992377.

Fax: 0266111701.
E-mail: servizio.clienti@coats.com

JAPAN
Puppy-Jardin Co. Ltd.,
3-8 11 Kudanminami, Chiyodaku,
Hiei Kudan Bldg. 5F, Tokyo.
Tel: (81) 3 3222-7076.
Fax: (81) 3 3222-7066.
E-mail: info@rowan-jaeger.com

KOREA
Coats Korea Co. Ltd., 5F Kuckdong
B/D, 935-40 Bangbae-Dong,
Seocho-Gu, Seoul.
Tel: (82) 2 521 6262.
Fax: (82) 2 521 5181.

LEBANON
y.knot, Saifi Village, Mkhalissiya
Street 162, Beirut.
Tel: (961) 1 992211.
Fax: (961) 1 315553.
E-mail: yknot@cyberia.net.lb

LUXEMBERG
Same as Belgium.

MEXICO
Estambres Crochet SA de CV,
Aaron Saenz 1891-7,
Monterrey, NL 64650.
Tel: +52 (81) 8335-3870.

NEW ZEALAND
ACS New Zealand, 1 March Place,
Belfast, Christchurch.
Tel: 64-3-323-6665.
Fax: 64-3-323-6660.

NORWAY
Coats Knappehuset AS,
Pb 100 Ulset, 5873 Bergen.
Tel: (47) 55 53 93 00.
Fax: (47) 55 53 93 93.

PORTUGAL
Apartado 444, 4431958 Vila Nova
de Gaia. Tel: (351) 2237 70773.
Fax: (351) 2237 70705.
E-mail: elvira.castro@coats.com

SINGAPORE
Golden Dragon Store,
101 Upper Cross Street #02-51,
People's Park Centre, Singapore
058357. Tel: (65) 6 5358454.
Fax: (65) 6 2216278.
E-mail: gdscraft@hotmail.com

SOUTH AFRICA
Arthur Bales PTY, P.O. BOX 44644,
62 4th Avenue, Linden 2104.
Tel: (27) 11 888 2401.
Fax: (27) 11 782 6137.

SPAIN
Oyambre, Pau Claris 145,
80009 Barcelona.

Tel: (34) 670 011957.
Fax: (34) 93 4872672.
E-mail: oyambre@oyambreonline.com
Coats Fabra, Santa Adria 20,
08030 Barcelona.
Tel: 93 2908400. Fax: 93 2908409.
E-mail: atencion.clientes@coats.com

SWEDEN
Coats Expotex AB, Division Craft,
Box 297, 401 24 Göteborg.
Tel: (46) 33 720 79 00.
Fax: (46) 31 47 16 50.

SWITZERLAND
Coats Stroppel AG, Stroppelstrasse
16, CH-5300 Tungi (AG).
Tel: 056 298 12 20.
Fax: 056 298 12 50.

TAIWAN
Cactus Quality Co. Ltd., P.O. Box 30
485, Taipei.

Office: 7Fl-2, No 140, Roosevelt Road,
Sec 2, Taipei.
Tel: 886-2-23656527.
Fax: 886-2-23656503.
E-mail: cqcl@m17.hinet.net

THAILAND
Global Wide Trading,
10 Lad Prao Soi 88, Bangkok 10310.
Tel: 00 662 933 9019.
Fax: 00 662 933 9110.
E-mail: theneedleworld@yahoo.com

UK
Rowan, Green Lane Mill,
Holmfirth,
West Yorkshire HD9 2DX,
England.
Tel: +44 (0) 1484 681881.
Fax: +44 (0) 1484 687920.
E-mail: mail@knitrowan.com

author's acknowledgments

I would like to take the opportunity to thank the following: Kate Buller of Rowan yarns for the opportunity to do this book; all the designers for their wonderful designs; the team of editors, designer, photographer and stylists who put the book together so beautifully; Penny Hill for her skill and her lovely knitters; Joy, Ruby and Mary for knitting for me; Sue Whiting and Emma King for pattern writing and checking respectively; and, last but not least, Mum for her invaluable help in finishing off garments and Dad for aving a much needed glass of wine on the table for me!